The Keys Against the Enemy

The Keys Against the Enemy

GINA R. PRINCE

CREATION HOUSE

The Keys Against the Enemy by Gina R. Prince
Published by Creation House
A Charisma Media Company
600 Rinehart Road
Lake Mary, Florida 32746
www.charismamedia.com

Cover design by Judith McKittrick Wright

Visit the author's websites: drginaprince.com, myhealthnsoul.com, and TheKeysAgainsttheEnemy.com

Library of Congress Control Number: 2017940071
International Standard Book Number: 978-1-62999-211-2

E-book International Standard Book Number:
978-1-62999-212-9

First edition

17 18 19 20 21 — 987654321

Printed in the United States of America

Introduction

I ***began writing this devotional*** because of a hunger I had for more of God. I wanted Him to pour into me everything possible to help keep me in His will. I was thirsty for encouragement on a daily basis. I knew I had to go to Him to get what I needed. I prayed for Him to guide me in the revelation and wisdom only He could give. As I began to write He revealed to me the need for this to be released for others to benefit from.

This devotional is for those who are looking for more. At the end of the next ninety days you will know you are more than a conqueror, an overcomer, and a winner! You are a warrior! You will be restored, equipped, and empowered to fight the demonic forces of the enemy on a daily basis. After reading this book you will feel victorious.

If you are faithful to stay in the Word and keep up with these devotionals you will grow in His wisdom and knowledge. You will begin to transform in your understanding. Your mind will be renewed. You will mature in the will of God. Your prayer life will increase, going to a higher level. This book will give you guidance and confirmation. You will become more confident in the things of the kingdom of God. Your faith will increase. God says He will give you strength, and this devotional will strengthen you in your belief that you can do all things through Christ and that there is nothing too hard for God.

I am so excited for your future. This ninety-day spiritual boot camp is the beginning of a new season in your life. I take authority against everything that would try to distract you on your journey. I cancel every work of the enemy to block or hinder your spiritual growth, in Jesus' name. I decree an increase of God's power and authority in your walk with Father in the name of Jesus, and no weapon formed against you, your family, finances, health, or anything else that concerns you shall prosper, in Jesus' name. I bind backlash and retaliation in the name of Jesus. May God's angels be encamped all around you, in Jesus' name. Amen.

This is your time of restoration, replenishment, renewal, transformation, empowerment, deliverance, breakthrough, and healing! It is your time to get your inheritance, every promise God has given you. As you journey through this devotional over the next three months you will begin to position yourself to receive all of the above and so much more. God has released what you need in *The Keys Against the Enemy* to walk in faith and authority every day. God bless you, and enjoy!

Day 1

Hungry?

Are you hungry? The Lord said that He has prepared a table for us in the face of our enemies (Ps. 23:5). Have you been to the table? God said He will supply all of our needs (Phil. 4:19). Do you let Him?

We have to get tired of doing it all by ourselves. The lie of the world is that we don't need anybody, and this is far from the truth. We need somebody; we just need to find the right somebody, and that somebody is Jesus. We cannot do it alone. We need Him in all things.

Some would argue that you can't have a relationship like that with Him. I say, "Why can't you?" I know that a relationship with God can give you comfort when you need it. Why? Because the Bible says He will send us a Comforter (John 14:16). God is a Father that cannot lie (Titus 1:2).

Also, a relationship with the Lord will give you peace. The Bible says the Lord will give you peace that will surpass all understanding (Phil. 4:7). A relationship with God will give you wisdom (James 1:5). The Bible says if you will ask anything in Jesus' name He will give it to you (John 14:14). If you ask for wisdom He will give it to you. A relationship with the Lord will cause you to be prosperous. The Bible says, "Above all things I wish that you shall prosper in all things even as your soul prospers" (3 John 2, author's paraphrase).

These are the words that are alive in your Bible. Have you read them? Do you believe what He says in it? If your answer is yes, then this is the beginning of a beautiful relationship. He is waiting for you to trust Him and need Him. He will show Himself mightily in your life if you will just give Him the chance. He is like *no* other. There is none like Him. He is the only true and living God. He loves and cares for you more than you know. God bless you!

Day 2

Standing Our Post

God has really placed in my spirit the importance of the body of Christ standing on our posts. We have to be determined to stand no matter what. The devil's job is to knock us off of our post. What is our post? We are gatekeepers and watchmen for the kingdom of God. (See 1 Chronicles 9:17–27; 2 Kings 11:4–18.) We are to watch for the attacks of the enemy in intercessory prayer and fasting. Those who are called by His name have a job to do. We are to stand for God unmovable and sure of who we are in Him. We are to stand, and in standing we bring the kingdom of darkness down. This is the way the devil attempts to knock us out of our position, because if we are distracted we won't see him coming. Some people would argue that "it don't take all that." I would have to disagree; it takes all that and then some more of it.

We have become so very complacent in our walk. We take some of the Word and leave the rest behind. Jesus gave us a command, and that command was to cast out devils and heal the sick (Matt. 10:7–8). Wait! There is more. He also said to go out and make disciples, "baptizing them in the name of the Father, and of the Son, and of the Holy Ghost" (Matt. 28:19). This is the command of the Lord, and this is our daily contribution to God's Kingdom.

Get back on your post if you have gotten off, and stand. God is waiting on your *yes*. Will you say yes? Be encouraged, knowing that there is a God on your side, the only true and living God.

Day 3

What's on Your Mind?

What's on your mind? Are you bound by worry, stress, or the cares of the world? God said cast all of your cares on Him (1 Peter 5:7). Many believers today are still in a state of depression, suppression, and oppression. We are to be free in the mind as well as all the other parts of the body, for who the Son has set free is free indeed (John 8:36).

When God speaks, we are to listen and rest in the knowledge that He will do what He said He will do. If we are not hearing from God, maybe our minds are too cloudy to hear from Him. We have to do maintenance on ourselves. We have to make sure we are watchful of what enters into the gateway of our minds. We have to make sure we watch what we are seeing and hearing. We as humans tend to want to know what is going on, not just sometimes but most times. This is why the media is in great business. They give exactly what we want—a whole lot of worry. If there is something to worry about they give it to us.

We have to take everything to the Lord in prayer. We have to realize that we are in the world but not of the world. We have to stand strong in Him. God is the Author and the Finisher, meaning He knows everything. He is all knowing! And He is concerned about you! So whatever it is you may be going through, trust in Him, and He will bring you through. God is faithful to His own, and He said He will take care of you. Stop believing the devil and his lies. God said that He is the name above every name. What power is that! God's name is above your bills, your job, your health, your spouse, your children, your next president, and even above you. Remember whom you serve and stand on God's side, unmovable! Don't let the devil move you. Your God is bigger than any circumstance. Nothing is too hard for God! Be blessed, and take it to the Lord and give it to Him.

Casting all your care upon him; for he careth for you.
—1 Peter 5:7

Day 4

Waiting

God chose us before we were in our mother's womb.

Ever wonder why it takes us so long to find out who we are and what is our purpose in life? God already knew who we were before we were even conceived. God allows us to grow and make choices on our own. He gave us free will to decide which way we want to go. Will we go with Him, or will we go to the world?

God is so merciful, and His grace is everlasting. He allows us to choose which path we want to go, like the prodigal son. He had decided that he wanted to receive all of his inheritance right now. (See Luke 15:11–32.) How many have seen themselves in this situation? We want what we want when we want it. Most of us can't wait, are anxious, and have got to have it now. (See Philippians 4:6.) Even though waiting can be hard on our flesh, the Bible says that faith without works is dead (James 2:26). I believe this is part of God's plan to help us grow into leaning on Him. The fact of the matter is that anything not worth waiting for is just not worth having. Some people believe that they have waited a long time for things. I have to ask, Is it that you waited a long time, or in that time was it hard for you to wait?

The prodigal son learned a very hard lesson in his anxiousness. He ended up losing everything and ended up with the pigs. Everything fast isn't good. He wasn't ready for his inheritance, his promise from his father. God knows what is best for us. He has made us a lot of promises, and He will deliver on them all. If God said it, He will do it.

We have to be ready for the outpour. God wants us to be able to withstand the blessing. Everything He does is eternal. There is no turning back in His plan for our life. God wants us to move forward in our blessing from Him. He wants our blessing to increase, not decrease. The next time you feel yourself being impatient in your wait on the things of God, think on that. He is worth the wait! God bless you!

Be careful for nothing; but in every thing by prayer and supplication with thanksgiving let your requests be made known unto God.
—Philippians 4:6

~Day 5~

Press In

Jesus, the name that is above every name (Phil. 2:9)! He is the great Messiah! The Lord has been really dealing with me concerning the church and where we are in our faith in Him. God is takin' it back to the old school.

We have gotten lazy in our prayer life. Remember the days of tarrying. Now, for some of you youngins, this is when we used to pray until we sweated out a perm, and it was serious. The mothers wouldn't stop until they knew that our prayers had been answered. I remember this is how I started speaking in tongues. They wouldn't stop until I got my breakthrough. Thank God for the mothers and the old-time way. They didn't care about anything else but making sure God came and did what God does best, and that is whatever we were believing Him for. God has been telling me that if you are praying once a day, increase it to twice; and if it is twice a day, make it three times.

The Bible says to pray with all supplication and without ceasing (Phil. 4:6; 1 Thess. 5:17). I think of the lady with the issue of blood and how she pressed her way in—smelling like blood and yet still pushing her way through the crowd, no matter what the people said or thought. (See Mark 5:21–34.) We have gotten so cute in our pray, praise, and even in our deliverance. I don't know about you, but I have never seen a pretty demon.

I just believe we need to prioritize and put the kingdom of God first. We have to care more about getting more of Him. We have to be ready for the warfare and stop thinking that fighting the devil is a cute job. The lie is from the devil. The devil wants you to have all of these hindrances so it hinders your fight against him. The devil wants you to think you are operating in power when you just may not be. When you go before the Lord—blood, sweat, and tears, waiting and wanting a breakthrough—God will give you what you need to fight your enemy.

You've got to know like the mothers knew that they stepped on that devil's head. I still love hanging around with the mothers. I give them a salute today and say God bless them. They are the original warriors.

May we press in and take a stand, lay hold of the promise, and stand our ground in faith until we reach a breakthrough. It is time! God is releasing a big outpour, and I don't know about you, but I am looking forward to it. I am doing my part so God can do His. I pray that you follow my lead and do the same. Seek Him with all diligence. Do more and more and more. It really is going to take all that.

We love You, Lord, and thank You for teaching us Your way. May we become more diligent in the things of You. Continue to open our eyes, that we may be able to see clearly, in Jesus' name. We want to be more like You. Help us where we are weak, and God, we ask for more of Your strength in Jesus' name. We thank You in advance for the transformation, in Jesus' name. Amen.

I believe God is going to answer your prayer, and you will see a difference in your prayer life in Jesus' name.

Wherefore God also hath highly exalted him, and given him a name which is above every name.
—Philippians 2:9

Day 6

Loving Your Brother

Going through tough times can be rough. Have you consulted the only one who really cares? God is really concerned about you and all of your problems. In times like these we need all the support we can get. I thank God for the body of Christ. It was God's intent that we should be there for one another. As the world goes through its changes, we as the body of Christ should be strong in one another. There is no *I* in the body of Christ.

So many people have been hurt in life that they tend to be mistrusting, even in God's family. Let me make this clear: God has called us His children, joint heirs with Christ in His kingdom. We are family! Whether we like it or not, if we are God's family we have to be delivered into loving it. The Lord says for us to love our brother, and if our brother has a need we are to be there. (See 1 John 4:7–11; Hebrews 13:1; 1 Peter 2:17; and Romans 12:10.) We have to learn the basics on how the Lord feels about us becoming one in Him. This means we have to put down our hang-ups and allow God to deliver us into the love He wants us to have. We have to allow Him to teach us how to love.

We have to learn how to be Christlike. Just think, if Jesus thought about not liking any of us, where would we be? He picked up His cross and died to every mean thing that was said to Him and about Him. He knew the greater picture was to be a servant unto God. He wanted to do what was pleasing to His Father. The problem is, we don't reverence God, and we don't fear

Him enough, some not at all. We sit in the congregation quoting Scriptures and hating the brother or the sister sitting next to us. That is not pleasing to God. We have got some work to do.

We are to love our brothers and our sisters. If you are carrying the spirit of anger, frustration, bitterness, unforgiveness, and/or hate, you are in need of deliverance, and you can be healed. God wants to deliver you and set you free. Remember, whom the son has set free is free indeed (John 8:36). When you are redeemed through the blood of Jesus, you become a new creature; all things of old are passed away (2 Cor. 5:17). Your mind has to be transformed, renewed, and refreshed.

You don't have to be the way you have always been with Christ. God's got something new in store for you. Allow Him to transform you into greatness while loving your brother, all at the same time. You don't have to worry about them, the people that mean you harm or no good. Let God deal with them. He will fight for you. Keep your eyes on the prize. Stay focused on Him. He will deliver you into greatness. Just keep pushing for change in Him, and you will see.

Beloved, let us love one another: for love is of God; and every one that loveth is born of God, and knoweth God. He that loveth not knoweth not God; for God is love. In this was manifested the love of God toward us, because that God sent his only begotten Son into the world, that we might live through him. Herein is love, not that we loved God, but that he loved us, and sent his Son to be the propitiation for our sins. Beloved, if God so loved us, we ought also to love one another.

—1 John 4:7–11

~Day 7~

Who's Your Daddy?

W*ho's your daddy?* God is a Father to the fatherless (Ps. 68:5). He is everything that we need. If you are feeling lonely or abandoned, turn to the Lord in prayer. He will fulfill all of your needs. There are so many people in the church, as well as in the world, feeling like an abandoned child. God says He is here for you. He will take care of you and supply all of your needs.

Some people have not allowed God to become this close to them. I assure you, if you surrender to Him He will be everything you have lost, wanted, or dreamed of. God is the man! I love Him! He has been a mother, a father, and a friend. It takes time well spent with Him to know who He is.

You don't have to go through life feeling like an illegitimate child. God calls you His child, joint heir to His kingdom. Just take the time to get to know Him. I promise you He won't let you down.

A father of the fatherless, and a judge of the widows, is God in his holy habitation..
~Psalm 68:5

Day 8

Walking by Faith

The Bible tells us to walk by faith and not by sight (2 Cor. 5:7). Walking by faith in what you don't see can be trying, but the Lord promised us that He wouldn't give us too much we can't handle (1 Cor. 10:13). We have to start by asking God to open our eyes to see what He sees.

He wants our faith to be in Him. Who is He? Abundant! He said He would do "exceedingly" and "abundantly above all that we" can "ask or think" (Eph. 3:20). God said He wishes above all things that we prosper, even as our soul prospers (3 John 2). If we can believe it we can receive it. What we *must* do is focus on the positive and His goodness. God wants us to have it all—not some, but all. Isn't that awesome?

Walk by faith, even when all hell is going on around you. It is a daily walk of discipline and reading the Word daily. It is a must! We have to meditate on His Word day and night (Ps. 1:2). The Word will help us to maintain our stand when the storm comes blowing our way. We can believe in better and, even more so, we can have better. Get fed up with a mediocre life and try what God has. He has it all!

I want all that God has for me—all of it, not some of it. When He shows Himself one way, I want more. I believe Him for even more, no matter how things look around me. I love what He does for us. He wants us always to come before Him with great expectations. He wants to do what man can't do. He wants to be glorified and honored. Give Him a chance and walk that walk of faith. Remember, "without faith it is impossible to please him" (Heb. 11:6).

Day 9

While We Wait

What do you do with the promises of God? The Word says "faith without works is dead" (James 2:20). How about if you do just that—work your faith? I have come to realize that your faith isn't in the promise itself; it is in God. We get very excited about the things that God tells us, and we believe it. The Word says to write it down and make it plain and, though it tarry, wait, because it will happen just like it said in due season (Hab. 2:2-3).

The problem is the wait. We believe God, and we know that He is faithful. Yet, there are times when it feels like the promise is so close we can taste it. What do we do then? The answer is, we wait. The season has not yet come. Even in the time of waiting the devil will come in to get you off track. The devil's job is to get you to a place of discouragement and for you to give up on what God has said. The devil's job is to steal your hope for a better tomorrow. In times like these you need to increase your prayer life and surround yourself with godly relationships that you can trust.

It is not easy. It wasn't easy for Sarah and Abraham, nor was it easy for Noah. Yet they stood no matter what. The devil tried to play on their weaknesses also, but thank God for His mercy. God is faithful, and He will keep you from falling. He will do what He said and also protect you, all at the same time.

God wants us to accomplish the goals that He has set before us. We have to be wise as a serpent and harmless as a dove (Matt. 10:16). God wants us to be aware of our adversary. He does not want us to be blind to the devil's tactics. This is what the enemy does. If you think of war and any other opposition you will understand that your strategy is to get to where your target is, and their goal is to stop you. Think of a football game or any other sport; there is offense, and there is defense. Play to win. Get your inheritance! Get what God promised you. It's yours for the taking. Be bold and go get it. Though it tarry, wait! The Bible says wait! Wait, I say, on the Lord. Keep plowing in the field until you reap your harvest. It's coming.

But wilt thou know, O vain man, that faith without works is dead?
—James 2:20

Day 10

Stand on His Promises

What a day! Today is such a blessed day! God is a true deliverer! I think about all the stuff that God has done for me. I thank Him for the sacrifice of Jesus Christ. He has blessed me in many ways. I can't even count them all. Just sit back today and think about the goodness of God. I believe we as believers sometimes get off course worrying about the things of the world. We forget who is really in control. God said in His Word, "If I will take care of the sparrow and the lilies in the valley, why wouldn't I take care of you?" (Author's paraphrase. See Luke 12:22–34.)

I know He has been faithful in providing for you. Do you have a roof over your head, clothes on your back, shoes on your feet, and food on your table? In this day and time, with all we are experiencing in our nation, you know that you should give God thanks. (See Psalm 34.) He said He would do it; it may not be the way we want it or when we want it, *but God!* He is faithful in supplying all of our needs. He is always right on time, no matter what a situation may look like at the time. Yes, I said "at the time," because trouble doesn't last always.

We have to fight like warriors and take the devil out! If you don't like where you are, be grateful, because there is always somebody that may be a little or a lot worse than you. When you finish thanking Him, believe the Lord for more. Stand on the promises He has given us in His Word. Fight the fight of faith and tell the devil to take his hands off your stuff. Get mad at the devil, not God. God wants to give it to you, and the devil wants to take it from you. Remember, the devil thought he won when Jesus died on that cross, but oh no! God had a plan. God had a plan, and we win! So, I just have to thank God for bringing me out of the worst and into the best.

I hear the Lord saying, "Trust and believe in Me, because the best is yet to come." I hear the Lord saying, "There will be an outpour. My people must learn how to wait for the appointed time. Though it tarry, wait, for it comes. When it comes it will be like a mighty wave." I hear the Lord saying, "Like a takeover. The righteous are taking over." The Lord says we are to take over and take back what the devil has stolen. God says, "Don't grow weary in your wait. Remain steadfast; continue to grow, continue to mature, for your labor in well-doing is not in vain. Stay focused," says the Spirit of the Lord. "I am faithful, and I will deliver. Don't believe any of the devil's lies. I am in control. The devil seeks to move you out from your destiny. Know that I rule and reign. Know that there is none like me. I will deliver my people. Turn from the thoughts of the world, and let your mind be on the things of me. Allow your mind to be transformed and renewed. Turn away from your wickedness and allow me to do the work. Make your mind up this day who you will serve," says the Spirit of the Lord. Those that have an ear to hear, listen to what the Spirit of the Lord is saying.

And he said unto his disciples, Therefore I say unto you, Take no thought for your life, what ye shall eat; neither for the body, what ye shall put on.
—Luke 12:22

Day 11

Thankful

As you go forth today, take the time to remember just how good God has been. Remember to give Him thanks for all He has done for you. I know that there is not one soul on this earth that cannot think of at least one thing He has done for them. Find something to be thankful for. Give Him praise for it, and I believe He will even add more.

Some of us go through the rollercoaster of life. We may say to God, "If you get me out of this or that, I'll do this." We make a pact with the Lord, but then what? Something comes along, and we go right back on our word. Think about it, how thankful are we? Let's do things differently this time. Think about getting your life right with Him. We don't want to take the same stuff from this season of our life into the next.

If you have been in a backslidden state this would be a good time to consider giving your life to Christ. Show your thanks to God by surrendering your life to Him. God is good, and He is worth your life. I can't imagine my life without Him. If you are sick and tired of being sick and tired, consider saying the sinner's prayer. Give your life to Christ!

Lord, I repent of my sins, and I surrender my life to You today. I thank You for giving Your life for mine. I believe that You died, were buried, and You rose from the dead. I want You to come into my life. I want to be more like You, and I give my life to You. I receive salvation from You. Thank You for being my Redeemer, in Jesus' name. Amen!

If you have openly said this prayer you are born again! (See Romans 3:24; 10:9–10, 13.) Praise God, for you are now my brother or my sister through the blood of the Lamb, Jesus Christ Himself. God bless you, and have a wonderful, peaceful, and relaxing day in Christ.

That if thou shalt confess with thy mouth the Lord Jesus, and shalt believe in thine heart that God hath raised him from the dead, thou shalt be saved. For with the heart man believeth unto righteousness; and with the mouth confession is made unto salvation.
—Romans 10:9–10

Day 12

Do You Know You Have a Good Thing?

Do you know you have a good thing? Jesus is our good thing. The Word reminds us to "taste and see that the LORD is good" and His love is everlasting (Ps. 34:8). I love to think about the goodness of God. He has truly been good to me.

We as people tend to make things so difficult with theology and our analytical thinking. God says to come to Him like a child. To come to Him like a child would mean to come innocently before Him, without any preconceived ideas or selfish motivation. It simply means, keep it simple. You don't have to bring man-made wisdom to the Lord. You don't have to bring Him the right answer. He wants you to come as you are, the real you!

The problem is, most of us do not know who we are. Release yourself to Him and discover who you really are. Allow Him to unveil you. Don't be afraid; you just may be pleasantly surprised. God created us in His image, and that's a good thing (Gen. 1:27).

O taste and see that the LORD is good: blessed is the man that trusteth in him.
—Psalm 34:8

Day 13

Make a Joyful Noise

Psalm 100:1 says, *"Make a joyful noise unto the LORD!"* In the midst of hardship and in the midst of the storm, make a joyful noise unto the Lord. He is worthy to be praised no matter what is going on.

It is always when the heat is hot in your trial that the devil will come in with lies to tell you, you used to be better off. Please don't listen to him; he is a liar, and there is no truth in him. The devil wants you to believe the Lord has brought you out of the old into the new just to leave you worse off. Remember the Word of God; He said He will never leave you, nor forsake you (Heb. 13:5). Think about it, as the saying goes, that which did not destroy you can only make you stronger.

The Israelites wandered around the mountain complaining about what they used to have in comparison to what they had at the time. As they kept going around the mountain they got stronger and stronger. Those that stayed in the race made it, and those that did not stay didn't. Will you be determined to stay in and make it? It is hard to go through trials, yet Paul said he rejoiced as he went through his trials (Rom. 5:3). They made him stronger, and as he went through them God was perfecting him daily.

I don't know about you, but I thank God that He cares about the details of my life. Face it; He knows the count of every hair on the top of our head. Every detail He is concerned about. Who pays that much attention to us? Nobody but Him! Make a joyful noise unto the Lord for Him being such a perfect daddy. He wants us to stay in the race and walk in victory. That's how much He cares. Let us not complain but be glad that we are being perfected. There is no greater love than that.

Day 14

Allow God to Work in You

Changes can be difficult to accept. Do you fear change? Are you comfortable with everything staying the same? God is forever elevating and increasing. The Word says if God be for you who can be against you (Rom. 8:31). We have to believe that God always wants to take us to a better place in Him. To do that, we have to bind the spirit of fear. Fear can be very crippling and can leave you stagnant. Release yourself from the bondage of fear and allow God to take you to greater heights in Him.

Jesus said we would do greater works than He did (John 14:12). Since we know this statement from His Word is true, we have to see that we are not in a position to do greater works the way we are now. God wants us to be used to do great exploits for His kingdom; however, it will cost us something. We have to drink from the same cup as the Lord our Savior did.

God is transforming today. Will you allow Him to do the work in you? As you allow Him to purge out the things that are detestable, He will quickly replenish you with more of Him. He wants to transform us to be more like Christ. This is part of change. You can't be afraid of your Father doing a work in you. He will continue the good work which He has already started if you continue to allow Him to (Phil. 1:6). The Bible says He will not withhold any good thing from us (Ps. 84:11). In other words, change can be good. Why try to have control over change? He is in control, whether you want to accept it or not. Increase your faith and trust in Him.

The best thing to do is to bind and cast out everything that would hinder Him flowing freely in you. Get mad at the devil! Some of you are not mad enough at the devil, your enemy. Whether you want to believe it or not, you have an enemy. Don't give him any more of your time. Don't allow him to steal any more time from you. Let God do what He wants in you. Give up the control, because you are only fighting yourself. With God we win every time. Without Him, we lose. Believe me when I say He always has a better way, so don't fear change; embrace it. It's the best thing for you.

What shall we then say to these things? If God be for us, who can be against us?
—Romans 8:31

Day 15

God's Faithfulness

The Lord and His faithfulness. When we think that He may be finished with us He then surprises us with even more. He is the great I AM THAT I AM who is full of life (Exod. 3:14). He said He came that we may "have life" and life "more abundantly" (John 10:10). Wow! Abundant life. Do you realize if Jesus came so we may have life and life more abundantly, then He must have some great things in store for us?

We must realize that we serve a God that never sleeps nor slumbers (Ps. 121:3–4). He never stops moving for us, in us, and around us. We have a lot to do, a lot to receive, and a lot to see. He wants to reveal His abundance to us. He has big plans for His people, and He is going to do them all. When God says it, He will do it.

We have to mature into the promise. God wants us to be able to withstand all that He has for us. Are we able to count the cost? Jesus once made a decision to leave His mother and family so that He might be about His Father's business. God asked Abraham to give his promised son as a sacrifice to Him. Abraham was willing to go that extra mile for God. He wanted to do what was pleasing to the one and only God Almighty. When God saw that he was ready to count the cost at any cost, God told him to put the child down and not sacrifice him. Abraham was being tested, and he passed. Will we be able to do what the Lord asks of us?

Are we as open to give our last dollar if God asked us to, trusting that He will provide what we need when we need it? He is our Provider! He provided a ram in the bush for Abraham, and He will do the same for us. We have to learn how to truly sacrifice—and not the easy stuff, but the things that would challenge us.

God wants to challenge your faith, as He did with the apostles on several occasions. Read it in the New Testament. The Apostles had their faith challenged to help mature them. Believe that God is in control, not on some things but everything. Remember, He is always right on time, and He will come through for you.

And God said unto Moses, I Am That I Am: and he said, Thus shalt thou say unto the children of Israel, I Am hath sent me unto you.
—Exodus 3:14

Day 16

Worship the Lord in the Spirit

Worship the Lord in spirit and in truth. I will worship the Lord "at all times: his praise shall continually be in my mouth" (Ps. 34:1). I believe the Lord is taking the body of Christ into a new level of worship. I believe this worship is unrehearsed and flows by the leading of the Holy Spirit. I believe God wants the Holy Spirit to flow freely in the musician as well as the vocalist. God wants to sing through us. He wants to share His thoughts and His love through song.

We have to allow God to come into the churches and have His way. We think we are following order, but our order can mean shutting our Father out. We have to let go of some control and allow Him to operate in the things He loves. We all know by reading His Word He loves worship and He loves to be praised. We shut Him out by going along with the protocol and not the Holy Ghost flow. When we open up to Him in our worship as worship leaders He will bless us prophetically in song.

I have seen and experienced Him minister to His people through song, unscripted and unrehearsed. Many people have been touched and delivered with opening up to Him this way. He opens up heaven right before our eyes. If we really want a revival we have to allow God and His anointing to come in more. As leaders we can't worry about everyone else's time; all we have to do is worry about God's time. We should know by now that God is always right on time. He can make you feel full in the same amount of time.

We just have to go to His table that He has prepared and stop trying so hard to put on a good show for people. Let God show Himself to the people. Let's be the vessels that He created. Sometimes a little is a lot with Him. If we put more time into calling out to Him and praising Him, I believe He will come in more. We don't always have to perform. All He wants to do is be invited more so He can show more of Him. He wants to do more for us. Tear the programs up and allow the Holy Spirit to come in and take our praise and worship to another level. We want to go into new dimensions and new heights in Him.

Praise and worship Him while you can and with every breath you have. Remember how the Lord used David to minister to Saul with his harp in song (1 Sam. 16:23). Read it; it will minister to you. The anointing of the Holy Spirit flowed through David's fingers into the soul of Saul. Let us release ourselves to the anointing of God in song, in our worship, and in our praise. Watch God turn your situations around at the same time, increasing your joy and peace.

I will bless the LORD at all times: his praise shall continually be in my mouth.
—Psalm 34:1

Day 17

What Can We Do?

Most of our lives we stand and watch for things to happen as if we are lifetime spectators. We often feel as though if it is not in our backyard then it has nothing to do with us. As we go forth we need to acknowledge just how much we could have done and what we still can do. The Word says if we will humble ourselves and turn from our wicked ways then God will heal our land (2 Chron. 7:14). I believe God is saying, "I will heal your land, your finances, your crops, your health, your national economy, and the church."

God wants us to put our faith and prayers to work. The Bible says, "Faith without works is dead" (James 2:26). We have to assume responsibility in the body of Christ. Now is the time to rise up and take your positions. It is time to take a stand! Ask the Lord, What can I do to make a difference? Believe that whatever you ask Him for in His name He will do. If you ask this question I'm sure God will direct you. He wants to use us! The work is available, but the laborers are few (Matt. 9:37). Let us keep this one thing in mind: there is always something we can do. The Word says the prayers of the "righteous...availeth much" (James 5:16). Let us not believe that for one second, our labor is in vain. Believe God is hearing your cry.

We have to come together as a nation under God, unified and in one accord, ready to take this nation back. We have to be willing to fight corporately and not stand on the sidelines just being a spectator. Now is your time to let God show you who you really are. We are one nation under God, no matter what the world, false religion, or false doctrine says. Believe the report of the Lord. Believe in who is in control. Take a stand! This is your country, and there is something you can do. President Donald Trump has been elected in, and instead of watching and waiting for him to make all these changes, let's increase our prayer for him and his family. Let's back him up in prayer. That's what he really needs. God is the one who will make the changes, starting right in our own back yard.

If my people, which are called by my name, shall humble themselves, and pray, and seek my face, and turn from their wicked ways; then will I hear from heaven, and will forgive their sin, and will heal their land.
—2 Chronicles 7:14

Day 18

A Change Is Coming

The Lord has laid it upon my heart this morning to really pray for the singles in the body of Christ. You may be going through a divorce or separation, but God wants you to know He is in control. God wants you to seek Him in all things, not allowing yourself to operate through your emotions.

There are some women and men that have been abused mentally, sexually, and physically. God knows what you are going through or what you have been through. He wants to heal you and deliver you. You are not damaged goods. Everything that has been broken, God can heal. Remember who is in control. The devil may have gotten a blow in, but God is doing a takeover. God said that vengeance is His (Heb. 10:30). He will curse those that have cursed you and bless those who have blessed you (Gen. 12:3). Don't worry about the oppressor. Keep your focus on God and allow Him to set you free. You are free in Him. Let Him shower you with His love. What you have to do is forgive no matter what and pray for them. Read the Book of Job. Job prayed for those who were around him that operated in ignorance, and God rewarded him for all he had lost because of his willingness to pray and forgive them.

To all my single people, keep your head up. It's not over until God says it is over. You are not alone. Single parents, keep your head up; God's got you. Allow God to do the work in you. Allow Him to help you through the process. He is processing you to present you. He has a plan for you. Keep your focus on Him.

The Bible says if you seek the kingdom of God first "all... things shall be added unto you" (Matt. 6:33). He said "*all* things" (emphasis added)! Remember that God's got this. Don't fall into self-pity. Say no to the devil's tactics. Don't allow him to play on your emotions.

Bind the spirit of lust, loneliness, depression, broken focus, sabotage, anxiousness, worry, doubt, disbelief, weariness, fantasy, fear of being alone, fear of rejection, rejection, Jezebel, witchcraft, and warlocks in Jesus's name. Pray and seek God diligently. He will come through for you. He knows how much you can bear.

Don't settle for anything. We are royal priests in God's kingdom, joint heirs with Christ (1 Pet. 2:9). Don't compromise. Stake your claim, and stand your ground. God's plan for your life is abundant, and it is everlasting, so don't give up the fight. Too many have fallen into this trap, only to get themselves off track and out of position. God says He works everything out for good (Rom. 8:28). He works everything out. This means He has lined up your mate for you; He will line your mate up with the assignment on your life. Stand still and wait on the Lord. I promise you, you ain't missing a thing.

Hold on for the great prize; it's coming! God says it is coming! He heard your cry, and He has seen what you have gone through. He says, "You have persevered. Now your reward comes. I do a quick work in your circumstance. Your season of change has come," says the Spirit of the Lord.

Take everything in prayer. Find out the strategy He has for you. Believe and trust God. See your miracle come through. It is on its way!

And I will bless them that bless thee, and curse him that curseth thee: and in thee shall all families of the earth be blessed.
—Genesis 12:3

Day 19

Faith

As I woke up this morning at 4:00 am and again at 5:00 am, the Lord spoke to me and said, "Let them know where I stand and where they stand with me." He says that even in these times He really wants those who have an ear to hear, to hear what the Spirit of the Lord is saying.

God says His people perish "for lack of knowledge" (Hosea 4:6). Romans 10:17 (NKJV) tells us, "Faith comes by hearing, and hearing by the word of God." Simply put, He said to "walk by faith, not by sight" (2 Cor. 5:7). He says He is in control. He is our Protector and our Provider.

He is reminding us we are in the world but not of the world. The Lord has given us a different kind of speech. We are to decree His Word. Death and life are in the power of our tongues (Prov. 18:21). Even in the middle of the storm the body of Christ has the power to speak life in any circumstance. We are to be the peculiar people God has created, set apart. We as the body of Christ don't have to be like the world. We don't have to say the same things; we don't have to look the same or act the same. We are set apart.

We need to operate in the power that He has for us and not tolerate any of the devil's nonsense. Even if God's hand is in this famine, remember that His Word will be tested, so let's pass the test and move on into the next level of the gift of faith.

God wants us to believe in Him no matter what. Believe His report. As long as you continue to do your part, God will always do His. He is faithful. Plead the blood of Jesus over all you have, and let God get rid of all that you don't need. He is doing a purging, cleansing, and shifting. Everything that stands during this process is good. Be encouraged this day.

Day 20

Standing on the Frontlines

Are you ready? Are you ready for a new and fresh experience in the Lord? It is time for a change, and that change starts within each and every one of us.

Change is good! It's a great thing to allow God to mold you into perfection daily. He is the Potter, and we are the clay. Wow! What an awesome experience in Him. I urge each and every one of you to allow God to reveal your hindrances and the things that are blocking you from your full potential. I believe God will show you truth and reveal strategies to overcome the obstacles that have been set before you to hinder you and ultimately try to destroy you. This is what the enemy does. Your opposer only does what he does best. This is the best time for you to be determined to win. Don't fold, and definitely don't lay down and die. Take it, pick it up, and walk that walk of strength and power in the Lord. Remember who your Daddy is. Remember that He wants nothing but the best for you.

It ain't over; it has only just begun. God is not done with the work He has planned for you yet. Eyes have not seen and ears have not heard all that the Lord has in store for you (1 Cor. 2:9). Are you still on the frontlines? Are you still willing to pick up your cross? Are you still willing to count the cost? Is your *yes* still *yes*?

Be ready to change; be ready to sacrifice; be ready to move when He says to move. It's alright! The change God has is good. Oh, boy, is it good, because the God we serve is good.

Day 21

No More, Devil!

Whenever you think of giving up, remember who is in control. God has the final say in everything. Don't allow yourself to step in and mess with what God is doing in your life through your situation. God is doing a work in His people. He wants us to be strengthened in Him. He wants us to walk in power through the blood of Jesus. We have to remember God gave His only Son so that we may have life and power. Jesus conquered death. If He conquered death and we are joint heirs to the kingdom of God, we have to understand that we are expected to seek after God's abundance and His power.

It is going to take authority and power to fight the demonic forces that are arising against God's people in this day and time. *No more playing church!* It is time to take a death walk of the flesh and truly seek the Lord on where we are weak. We have to cut the heads off the hydra, the reoccurring curses that continue to keep coming back in our lives to wreak havoc. We have to say, "No more, devil! You and your demon soldiers have got to go in Jesus' name!" Be determined not to give the devil anything, starting today. If you want a breakthrough, a Red Sea breakthrough, then every door must be closed to the past. You have to make your mind up today. This is a right-now request from the Lord that is pleasing to Him. He is not pleased with seeing His children compromise to the devil.

God says we don't have to be beaten anymore. He wants us to rise up out of the dead state and become the real soldiers He created us to be. Stand and be determined not to fall back again. Face the devil head on; stop running and hiding. It's time-out for the church being scared of the devil. It's time-out for pretending and faking it through. We have got to get real with it and be determined to fight. Freedom does cost you something, but thank God we didn't have to pay the price that Jesus did.

Yet, we will have to pay a cost to live the way Christ did. We want the power, but there are many that don't believe it will have to take all that. I surely hate to burst the bubble of those who believe that lie. It is going to take all that, this, and then some—and some more of that. We have to come out from the spoiled child syndrome and persevere so that when we persevere we will mature (James 1:2–4). We have to be mature solders. This should be our goal daily. The greater works Jesus said we would do than He did will cost us our life as we know it. We will have to allow God to do the work that needs to be done. This is what is required for the operation of miracles, signs, and wonders. We are talking about the power of the blood of Jesus and walking in governmental authority in Jesus' name. This is who we really are.

Old saints, don't let the new children pass you by. There is still yet more for you to do. You may be growing older in the natural, but God says you are much younger in the spirit. Think about Abraham and Sarah.

Are you ready for this? I pray for you to have a made up mind and get ready for a journey of transitioning into handling your Father's business in the power that is ordained for you. Be blessed in Jesus' name.

My brethren, count it all joy when ye fall into divers temptations; Knowing this, that the trying of your faith worketh patience. But let patience have her perfect work, that ye may be perfect and entire, wanting nothing.
—James 1:2-4

Day 22

Praise Him

Today is a new day! As we walk through the valley of the shadow of death, we will fear *no* evil (Ps. 23:4). It doesn't matter what you have been going through; if you look around you, you will see you are still functioning, and yes, you have survived up to this point. You have made it through. You have overcome to get to where you are now.

If you are still standing you need to praise God. Give Him praise right where you are. I don't know about you, but when I think about what He has brought me through this year I can't help but praise Him. God is worthy of praise, honor, and glory not just today but every day! We made it! We made it! And guess what? God is not finished with us yet.

This may sound religious to some, but I tell you we can never get rid of the foundation that has brought us to where we are today. God has built us on a solid foundation, and it's OK to go back to the old-time way every now and again. The old ways won't totally help where this world is today, and that is OK. God continues to equip us for the new battles every day if we let Him. He is more than equipped to give the body of Christ what we need in this season, but there is nothing wrong with taking it back every now and again.

It is never over until God says it is over. It may have been rough this past season of your life. You may have cried hard and may have hurt hard, but you made it this far! By God's grace you made it. I believe God for a release in this next season. I believe with all the purging and the shifting we have endured as the body of Christ we are now in position for the outpour of God's beautiful glory. I believe Him for more signs and wonders, children preaching the Word and saying, "Thus says the Lord..." I believe that we will see more of the impossible becoming more possible.

I advise you to stay connected. Ask God to give you more wisdom and more discernment. I pray for you more strength and endurance. Remember, if you made it through this far, there is nothing you cannot do through Christ Jesus, who strengthens you.

Yea, though I walk through the valley of the shadow of death, I will fear no evil: for thou art with me; thy rod and thy staff they comfort me.
—Psalm 23:4

~Day 23~

Confusion

Stay out of the trap of confusion. The devil is being very busy in setting up the traps of confusion. There are these shadows the Lord has revealed to me in a vision that are not of Him. The Lord says these shadows are of the adversary. The Lord says the devil is attempting to overshadow the promises God has made to His people. The Lord says the devil is attempting to discourage us with these shadows. If he can get away with it, then the promises God has made to us will be stolen.

We have to remain on guard and very watchful against this silent attack of the enemy. Bind off the spirit of blindness and anxiousness in Jesus' name. Bind off the spirit of confusion in Jesus' name. Ask God to give you wisdom and clarity. I pray in Jesus' name you will remain faithful to the things God has asked of you and that you do not surrender to the enemy's tactics. Remember whom you serve and remain obedient to the end. It is not over until God says it is over. God will let you know what is of Him and what is not. Don't move too quickly, because things that present themselves may sound and look good but are not.

Be aware and take heed to the words that I speak to you today. It will save you time and unwanted consequences in the long run. Only desire to be satisfied in Him. Don't settle for anything less.

...remain on guard and very watchful against this silent attack of the enemy.

Day 24

Wait on God's Direction

Waiting on the Lord's direction can be hard. Our first instinct is to move and move quickly. The Word of the Lord says wait, "wait, I say, on the Lord" (Ps. 27:14). We have to learn to be patient in waiting. We also have to learn how to move when He says to move. Some of us wait too long and miss the mark. What, then, do we do? We wait and learn to lean on the Lord and trust He will guide us through our next level. We have to trust Him to lead us in the way we should go. It may be hard, yet this is the beginning of our fleshly death walk.

The death walk of the flesh is a must when we are following the leading of the Lord. We tend to want to have everything figured out and worked out, yet with walking with the Lord we have to surrender all that. We have to grow in faith and trust in Him to lead us to victory. Yes! We are victorious even in the mess. We have won, even though it may not look like it. We have to call those things that "be not as though they were" (Rom. 4:17). Stand and wait even when it is hard. Stand and wait even when it is looking bad. Stand and wait on God to bring it all together for you in Jesus' name.

Wait on the Lord: be of good courage, and he shall strengthen thine heart: wait, I say, on the Lord.
—Psalm 27:14

Day 25

Climb Your Mountain

As I was sitting back wondering and allowing the Holy Spirit to lead me in the way I should go in writing the daily word for the day this question came to my spirit: Is there anything too hard for God? The Bible tells us no, there is nothing too hard for God. Can we say this as we are faced with challenges? I have had a few in my time with serving the Lord. It would seem at times the challenges get harder and harder. As soon as I make it through one victoriously, here comes another.

In prayer one morning—as I go before the Lord every morning daily before I even leave the house—I sought Him for my daily portion of strength and direction. He spoke to me and said, "Every obstacle you overcome takes you to the next step." With this in mind I realized something. I realized these challenges are like steps that take us higher and higher in Him. We actually are climbing the mountain. I think about how Moses had to climb the mountain to get to God. Do we really know how hard it is to climb a real mountain? I am sure Moses faced challenges on the way to the top, possibly bad weather conditions, maybe some kind of mountain animal. God allows our way to be challenging to strengthen us.

A victorious life requires discipline and hard work. As the saying goes, no pain; no gain. Even though we go through some rough places to get closer to our Father, He is very faithful in keeping us from falling. For this we should be forever grateful. I thank God today for the strength and the endurance He has given me. I can honestly say I feel like a champion. I am a winner, and so are you.

Keep pushing up. Don't fall back to the devil, and you will receive your reward, a reward like no other: more of Him! Know God is able to carry you through. Believe God can do all things and there is nothing too hard for Him. He can bring you through anything if you let Him. Allow Him to show you the way up your mountain. Allow Him to give you the strategy to make it over. Remember you are a winner.

Challenges are like steps that take us higher and higher in Him. We actually are climbing the mountain.

Day 26

The World Isn't Winning; We Are!

Who are we really in Christ? Sometimes it seems as if the world has things all figured out. It even seems at times they are happier than we are. This can be a little discouraging and even cause us in the body of Christ to question, What is all the sacrifice for? We may even ask God, Can we get more of you to show the world we have been sent and there is a difference? The difference should show more of His glory in us.

This can be a little challenging in our walk. To be faithful in the things of God is to believe Him when He says that we are more than conquerors, we are ambassadors, and we are victorious. We not only have to believe this but also have faith in this. Yes! It can seem as if the world is winning when we look at this world in the natural. We have to look with our spiritual eyes and know the devil is a liar. When we start looking at the things in the world and start feeling like we are missing something, these are the lies of the tempter.

We have to bind off the spirit of the tempter and the spirit of lies. These lies are told to us to get us off track and to tempt us to go back to doing things the world's way. We don't have to! We have the power through the blood of Jesus to live a powerful, victorious, and healthy life in Jesus. We can have peace, joy, and fun. We can have healthy marriages and pretty cool children. The world may act like they have it all together, but please believe this is only an illusion. What would have been the purpose of Jesus dying on that cross? He gave His life so the world could be set free. He came that we may have life, and life more abundantly (John 10:10). This is His promise to us.

We may feel discouraged at times, yet we have to really remember at these times who we are. We are the children of God, joint heirs with Christ. He is rich, and so are we. We can have it all. God promised us He would do "exceedingly abundantly above all that we ask or think" (Eph. 3:20). Even though we know there is no life without Christ, remember this especially when the devil tries to tempt you. We have to resist the devil, and he will flee. If this is not enough, start calling out the demons that have been sent to distract you. If this is not enough, run. Paul said sometimes you have to run. (See 1 Corinthians 6:18, AMP.) Move on, and stop hanging around the people, places, and things where you are weak. Stop hanging around single folks that are not serving the Lord. This is how you win—and we *are* winners.

Stand your ground in the Lord and let the world know who you are. You are somebody truly special. You are anointed to fight against principalities, strongholds, and spiritual wickedness in dark places. *Victorious* is who you are! You are not missing a thing, because you have everything in Christ. He is everything!

The thief cometh not, but for to steal, and to kill, and to destroy: I am come that they might have life, and that they might have it more abundantly.
—John 10:10

Day 27

The Strength of Singleness

The Lord gave me this revelation on January 8, 2009: "A single person can chase one thousand and two can put ten thousand to flight (Deut. 32:30)."

The Lord also revealed to me the challenges of being single compared to being in a marriage. It's harder to maintain as a single, because we are going at it alone. When you are married you have the two that can lean on one another. When it is one you have to learn to lean on the unseen but very well-known Jesus Christ. It is easier for a married person to call on their husband or wife to pray for them when they are tired or have sex to get some temporary release. When you are single you have everything to fight up against. You have the natural tendencies of being human. You can't get any sexual release. You have to be disciplined all the way through.

We as singles have the natural body parts that function as God has created them to. God said it is not good for man to be alone (Gen. 2:18). Paul made reference to this in the New Testament (1 Cor. 7:9). As singles we have to fight up against the battles that come up against our loins. We have to be strong in the lonely hour. We have to fight up against being targeted from the enemy in all areas of our mind, body, and spirit. There is always a war going on to take our souls, and in all of this we have to lean on and depend on God to get through it. This can be difficult, and this is why discipline is a must—daily exercises, I call it.

Marriage is great, and most single people look forward to getting there. Being single can be great, yet we have to have a made-up mind to be steadfast until God sends our mate. All and all, be encouraged, you who are single. God has you there because He knows you can handle it. It takes great strength to be single, and it shows you have a lot of fight in you. It is all how you look at things.

Regardless of whether you are married or single, as people we were created to be in relationships from the very beginning. We are asked to love our brothers and sisters, to encourage one another, and also we are a people that are part of one body. We are to function as one body, working together to help build the kingdom of God.

God is renewing the mind-set of His people so we can know the truth. He wants us to know the devil is really afraid of a steadfast, unmovable single person who is fighting him on a daily basis. God wants us to know that when the time is right and our mate comes we will both know we have gone through the same process. This is why it is very important for us to wait on God to send our mate. What God puts together no man can "put asunder" (Mark 10:9).

God wants us to learn not only how to be end-time warriors while single but also to be end-time warriors when we are together in matrimony. He is a jealous God, and He does not want us to get lost in the relationship; instead, the relationship will be an addition to us. This means more of one—which, in marriage, is two—means more power. His desire is that we don't come all this way just to throw in the towel once we enter into marriage.

Think about it and be encouraged, because He truly knows what we are going through. He promised us He wouldn't give us too much we couldn't handle. He is faithful like that. Trust God to do what He needs to do in your single life. The double portion you receive for your faithfulness will be worth the wait, and at the end of the day this is why the devil wants us to give it up so easily. Gird your loins, put on your breastplate, and stay on the battlefield. We win! I believe the sooner we get this the sooner our promise will come. I believe your mate is waiting for you just as much as you are waiting on them. Just align your heart with God and keep your focus on Him in spirit and in truth.

Day 28

During the Wait

Waiting on the manifestation of your promises can be long and hard, but don't get hard in your wait. Some people become bitter and resentful in their wait. Believe me, God knows the heart and thoughts of man. Look at this wait as an opportunity to grow and mature. There is no time like this to build a closer relationship with the Lord. Take more time to pray and seek His face for comfort and peace in your wait. Your manifestation is on its way. Remember, it is not how long you wait; it is how you wait. Stay focused on the prize. God will deliver. Don't allow yourself to become hard. This is not what God had intended for you. Dwell in His perfect peace, for He is truly there for you.

> But they that wait upon the LORD shall renew their strength; they shall mount up with wings as eagles; they shall run, and not be weary; and they shall walk, and not faint.
>
> —Isaiah 40:31

Look at this wait as an opportunity to grow and mature.

Day 29

Supernatural

To receive a supernatural blessing you must think supernaturally. This is the year of supernatural manifestation, and this is your year of the increasing of your faith to believe in the supernatural things of God. Remember, "faith cometh by hearing, and hearing by the Word of God" (Rom. 10:17). You must hear the Word, you must study the Word, and you must do what the Word says.

This is the year of much-given, much-required (Luke 12:48). We have to be prepared to get the unexpected. We have to be prepared for God to ask of us to do the unexpected. I believe God is taking the church out of the ordinary into the extraordinary. God is challenging the church to believe in the impossible. He is bringing us out of settling for less into expecting more. He is bringing forth a people who will be obedient unto death, for obedience is greater than sacrifice (1 Sam. 15:22).

This is the year for the real believers to please stand up. It is time for the soldiers and the generals to rise up. Those who have been warring in the spirit for His kingdom behind the scenes, this is your year for breakthrough. God is doing a new thing. Get ready for this outpour. Get ready to receive an overflow. "This is your year," says the Spirit of the Lord. The time is now.

So then faith cometh by hearing, and hearing by the word of God.
—Romans 10:17

Day 30

All or Nothing

All or nothing! God says He wants all. He wants all of your heart, body, and soul. He wants you to have more of a desire for Him and nothing else. He wants your love and your thoughts.

Are you willing to give Him His desires? We always want to know about Him giving us *our* desires, but are we ready and willing to give Him His? Before you think of asking Him for another thing—as if He hasn't been good enough to us already—ask yourself, What am I willing to give up? Even if you feel you have nothing else to give and you are on the brink of giving up, please just hold on and ask God to help you, because you really do want to give Him your all. He will do it for you. He just wants you to want what He wants. He wants your covenant with Him to be two-way, not one-way. (See Deuteronomy 6:5; Matthew 6:33.)

He just wants you to want what He wants. He wants your covenant with Him to be two-way, not one-way.

~Day 31~

Don't Give Up

A fresh anointing is very needed in the body of Christ. We need for God to give us some relief. In your prayer ask God to give the refreshing you need. He says we "have not, because" we "ask not" (James 4:2). Believe He is the "rewarder of them that diligently seek him" (Heb. 11:6). We have to know He takes care of those who take care of His business. We have to maintain our stand with Him and know He will give us what we need when we need it.

God is stretching us and increasing us into greater levels in Him. Please remain steadfast and don't give up. Don't let the heat from the fire chase you away, but may it draw you closer to Him. Only God can bring us out of whatever it is we are going through. There is no greater love than His. He loves us so much He gave His only begotten Son. Lean on Him. He will deliver you, He will protect you, and He will keep you. He will not give you too much of what you cannot handle. He is faithful and generous in all of His abundance. That's the kind of God we serve. Get to know Him, and allow Him to show you His grace and His mercy in your life.

Ye lust, and have not: ye kill, and desire to have, and cannot obtain: ye fight and war, yet ye have not, because ye ask not.
~James 4:2

Day 32
Stimulate

Stimulate: 1. Excite to action; invigorate. 2. Quicken.

I heard this in my spirit, and I felt the Lord speaking to the church, saying, "It is time for the church to be stimulated into the position of defense. It is time to go on the defense." I heard the Lord saying the church has been sitting down and falling out of place for a long time now.

He is now doing a stirring in the spirit to awaken the church to stand up in an upright position. We have been lying down and allowing the devil to continue to take over. The Lord says, "We tend to believe we are taking it back from the devil, and yet we are not defending our positions, our churches, our children, or our nation. It is time to fight!" We have to really fight in the spirit; we have to learn how to stand against the grain. We have to learn that it is OK to be confrontational. We have to understand the Word says we will be disliked and rejected for His name's sake (John 15:8–21). We have to learn to take the risk of being rejected and mocked for Jesus. We have to be willing to count the cost.

This year we will definitely see the difference from the real and the fake. We will know by our spirit who is really on the Lord's side. We will know because God has a chosen remnant for this season to whom He has given this anointing. This remnant will be able to discern the truth and will truly have an awakening of what God is seeing.

God said He is coming for a bride without "spot, or wrinkle" (Eph. 5:27). God is not pleased with the way we have allowed the enemy to come in and infiltrate our gates. We have truly got to take our nation back. We have truly got to take it all back by force. We have got to be equipped to fight. We have got to humble ourselves and allow God to lead us into getting the training we are going to need for this type of warfare. We cannot allow fear to paralyze us into staying stagnated.

Seek the knowledge you will need, and stop allowing pride to stop you from learning. An unteachable spirit is one of the most hindering spirits. The Word says people perish from "lack of knowledge" (Hosea 4:6). Do you want yourself to be the cause of you lacking knowledge, which could ultimately help you in your spiritual walk?

Give this some thought, and continue to look to God for help. Jesus died for us to have this power. It is in His blood, so we are able to do all things. We fight principalities, not flesh and blood (Eph. 6:12). Remember who we are and what we were created for.

For we wrestle not against flesh and blood, but against principalities, against powers, against the rulers of the darkness of this world, against spiritual wickedness in high places.
—Ephesians 6:12

Day 33

Explosion

I saw what looked in the spirit to be an explosion. I heard the Lord say,

There comes an explosion. I am blowing up every man-built tower, like the Tower of Babel. [See Genesis 11:1–9.] I am blowing it all up. They must come down! Everything man has entrusted outside of Me must blow up and be gone. The focus must come back to Me.

Those who have stood by Me and not turned from Me, this is your year of increase, and in the blowup a transfer will take place. Everything that was stored up from man's worship in false gods and in idol worship will be dispersed to all of you. You will hear of more checks coming in the mail supernaturally, more property being transferred from one person to another supernaturally, and business deals working out in your favor—giveaways!

I urge you to stand your ground, and don't fall into temptations. Pray with all supplication. Set a goal concerning Me and stick with it. Be determined this year to receive spiritual breakthroughs. Go beyond what you have in the past. Go the extra mile in your time, talent, and tithing. The devil wants to take you out, and he is roaming to seek who he can take out. I tell you, his desire is to sift you as wheat. Be sure to stand, no matter what the urge or the trial; stand, and you will see My words come to pass.

Those that have an ear to hear, hear what the Spirit of the Lord is saying in Jesus' name. Amen.

Day 34

Trust in the Lord

"***Trust in" God with all of your heart***, and "lean not" on your "own understanding" (Prov. 3:5). The time is now, end-time warriors. The time is now to let go and let God. You have to put all of your trust and faith in Him. You have to trust God to do things the way He wants to do things. He is calling forth a remnant that is ready for battle. Let Him use you the way He wants to use you.

It is an honor to be used as a servant for God. See it this way, and He will guide you all the way. Things will not be done to your comfort. War is not comfortable. War is confrontational. We have to get out of fearing man and start to fear God. You have to reverence Him. You have to put Him first. It is not about pleasing man. You have to do what is pleasing to Him. Now is the time for the real soldiers to stand up. Are you a real soldier?

He has called forth the trailblazers, the pioneers, and the forerunners. We have got to move when God says to move. If we don't, we could get ambushed. Remember who your leader is. It is God almighty, and Jesus is with us. Get into position, and stand your ground.

Wake up, church! The devil is right at the gate, ready to ambush. Stop him! Pray, intercede, and stand in the gap. Now is the time. Catch up on the current events. Pay attention to the undercurrent of these events, because the focus is not just on the economy. Pay attention to the bills that are being passed. Pay attention to the laws. Pay attention to what our president is saying. Don't get caught up in one subject; study to show yourself approved. The enemy has an agenda. Wake up, church, and pay close attention. Ask God to give you discernment. Ask Him to lead you into things you should know. Be aware and stay focused. Now is the time for you to come forth. Dead men's bones, arise in Jesus' name!

~Day 35~

Nothing Is Impossible for God

"*Is there any thing too hard for*" *God?* (Jer. 32:27). There is nothing impossible for God, nothing too big or too small!

Now is your time to increase your faith and expand your trust in Him. He is the only one who knows all and is all. There is no one else. You can lean on and trust in Him to do everything and all things. This is the year of supernatural belief. Anything less than that will not do. This is the year of obedience and supernatural belief.

God is in control, and He rules and reigns. Try God this year. Make it a goal of yours to extend yourself to Him until you receive a breakthrough of new belief, fresh faith, and a steadfast walk with your Lord and Savior. He is real, no doubt about it! Stay focused on Him, in Jesus' name!

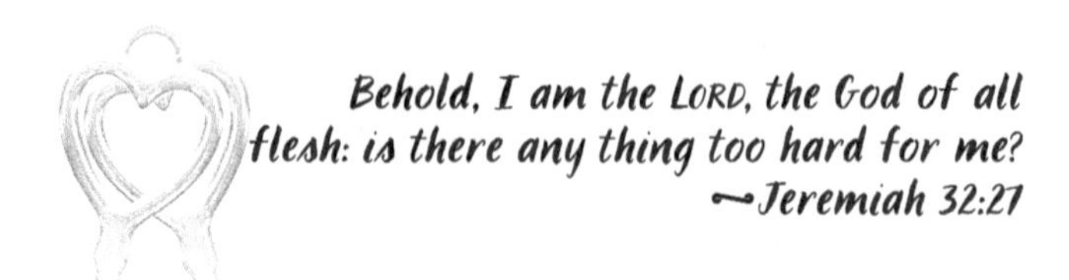

Behold, I am the LORD, the God of all flesh: is there any thing too hard for me?
—Jeremiah 32:27

Day 36

Your Help

Remember, your help comes from the Lord (Ps. 121:1–2). No matter what the trial, the storm, or the circumstance, God is your very present help. He will always be there in your time of need. He is there before you need, when you need, and after your need is met. He never sleeps nor slumbers. Remember where your help comes from. He is your Deliverer. He is your Keeper. He is your Source.

Don't let go of Him! Keep holding on. He will bring you through, and guess what? The key word is *through*. Going *through* means you will come out! Whenever you hear Him say, "I am bringing you through," that means you will come out. Faith comes by hearing the Word of God (Rom. 10:17). Praise God for the victory of coming out! Declare this today: "The storm is over now, in Jesus' name!" God is bringing you *out!*

I will lift up mine eyes unto the hills, from whence cometh my help. My help cometh from the Lord, which made heaven and earth.
—Psalm 121:1–2

Day 31

To Lose Is to Gain

Those who lose their life will gain one. We have to come to realize to live for Christ is to die to self. (The good news is that living for Christ is also "gain," according to Philippians 1:21.)

Everyone wants to discuss over and over again what the nation is undergoing. As important as the issues are, we have to keep it moving. We have to continue on in our walk and the duties the Lord has commanded us to do. We cannot let anything stop us. We have to keep it moving and not allow anything to distract us. We have to seek the Lord for more wisdom (Prov. 2:6). We have to continue to seek deliverance.

We have to count the cost at all costs. We may lose friends. We may have to move out of a city or a church. You must go to a church that will feed you and challenge you. You are looking for deliverance into your destiny. You are looking forward to becoming great and walking into excellence, virtue, holiness, and righteousness. It is time to be in the right place for the right time.

God is doing a great work in the church. There is a purging and a sanctification going forth. All is well when it makes things better. We have to believe and trust God to do whatever it will take to get our church ready for our Bridegroom. He said He is coming for a bride without "spot, or wrinkle," and this is the word of truth (Eph. 5:27). The bride must undergo some surgery, and we have to humble ourselves to the process. We have to count the cost. Be prepared, for God is making His rounds. His desire is that none should perish, so take note, get ready, and let the process of change begin.

Day 38

Transitioning from Old to New

As God transitions you there is always a required change. Change can be difficult for some and yet very rewarding at the same time. The transitioning part is most difficult because you never know how He is going to do it. We may say, "He normally does it like this with me," or "He has always done it like that," but even that can be changed. The fact of the matter is, God can do things any way He likes. We have to learn how to go with His flow.

Change from God is always good. He is always elevating and evolving. God has the best plan, and He knows what we need. God gives us what we need to fulfill His purpose. We have to die of ourselves and live with more of Him. We want the perfect will of God for our lives, and sometimes—if not most of the time—it is not what we want. We have to learn to trust God with our lives and allow Him to make all of the decisions. We cannot transform God; He can only transform us. We cannot control God; He is always in control. We must allow Him to take us to the level of excellence He desires for us to have. Allow God to transition you into His perfect will for your life and believe what He has is good, all good.

> For I am confident of this very thing, that He who began a good work in you will perfect it until the day of Christ Jesus.
>
> —Philippians 1:6, NASU

Day 39

When the Fire Is Hot

God has a plan for your life, and the gates of hell will not prevail against them. Learn to trust in the Lord, and "lean not on your own understanding" (Prov. 3:5, NKJV). He is your deliverer in a time of need. He will come through to cool you right off. Even if the timing is not right now for you to come out, know that you are coming out and that this is a time of refining in the heat. Believe you are coming out and trust God to bring you out.

Right now some of you may be going through what would appear to be a fiery hot transition. Some of you may feel like you have just been dropped off in the middle of hell. If you can relate to this, please wait on God. I think of Shadrach, Meshach, and Abednego. (See Daniel 3.) When the enemy turned that fire higher and higher they could do nothing but call on and depend on God. Because of their determination in trusting God, their Father was then able to deliver them right in the face of their enemies. Believe me, He is doing a purging in the heat, a cleansing in the heat. He knows exactly what you are going through, and He will deliver you, only this time you are coming out for good! Somebody really needs to praise God right there.

Will you choose to believe that this fire will ultimately bring you out from the things that hold you bound? They will be no longer, in Jesus' name! "You are free," says the Lord, and who the Son has set free is free indeed (John 8:36).

Day 40

Show Your Love for Him

What's next on the agenda?

We still have much work to do in the church. Seasons have changed, and time is going by. We have to get out, save some souls, and change some lives. The harvest is plenty, "but the laborers are few" (Matt. 9:37, NKJV). There is so much we can do individually and corporately.

We have to step out of the box. It is time to expand. This job we do for the Lord is 24/7. We should be doing what is pleasing unto Him, not ourselves. We should die of the flesh and allow God to raise us up into the position He has created us to be in. As we surrender our time and gifts to Him, He will open many doors. Don't allow fear to paralyze you. Get up and do something! This is your time!

God wants to expand your ministry. We know you love Jesus, but now is the time to show Him how much you love Him. How do you show Him how much you love Him? By loving on His people and expanding the kingdom. You show Him your love for Him by being obedient and multiplying. It is your time! Rise up to the call! You can do it! Know how I know? Because the Bible tells me so. Read it and allow it to speak to you. If you take care of His business, our Father will take care of you. The Bible says you "can do all things through Christ who strengthens" you (Phil. 4:13, NKJV). Now is your time! Need strength? He will give it to you. Go out and win some souls in Jesus' name!

Day 41

Open Heaven

Let our minds be clear and our hearts be opened to what God has in store for us.

It is time for the manifestation of what God has promised. I feel a clarity in my spirit that God is opening up the heavens even more upon the righteous who have followed Him and who have been diligent in serving Him. He is opening the heavens even more to pour out the overflow of supernatural rewards.

I can see an opening of light pushing away the darkness of clouds that seemed to have been hovering over the heads of the chosen in this season. This darkness has been to scatter the weak and the evil. This darkness has been allowed to strengthen those who have been alarmed, and the process of purging has been doing an ongoing deliverance in you. As this cloud is being removed, you are becoming stronger in the areas that have held you bound.

Some of you had no understanding what has been taking place, and you had no understanding where you were. God is bringing forth clarity and an understanding to you that will take you into a new level of maturity. Stay focused on your stand for the Lord, and you will see the fruit of your labor coming forth.

I felt an urgency to write this down as I was awakened from a nap. I really feel God is ready to do some amazing things in the face of the enemy. He is ready to release the blessings that have been stored up. He knows you have been faithfully waiting, and I hear the Lord saying, "The wait is over." He will make it clear and plain to you in your wait.

The Lord will open the heavens, the storehouse of his bounty, to send rain on your land in season and to bless all the work of your hands. You will lend to many nations but will borrow from none.

—Deuteronomy 28:12, NIV

God is bringing forth clarity and an understanding to you that will take you into a new level of maturity.

Day 42

Make a Decision

All glory to the King! We await His return, and we know the King is coming back. He is coming back, just like He said He would.

Are we ready? With all of the misinterpretation of the Word of God, have we forgotten God said He was coming for a bride without "spot, or wrinkle" (Ep. 5:27)? Have we become so consumed in our fleshly desires that we have become hardened to the truth and purposes of the gospel of Jesus Christ? It is time now that we as the body of Christ take a close and good look at our lives. We have to decide if we are really ready to sacrifice and lay down our lives for the kingdom of God. We have to take the time to put *all things* down that would hinder us from becoming purified under the cleansing power of the blood of Jesus. We have to make our minds made up to want to believe in the full gospel of Jesus Christ. We have to believe that we can live holy lives according to God's plan for our lives and stop using the excuses of the world to stay in the lust of the flesh. We have to desire more of kingdom living. We can do all things through Christ who will strengthen us, if we let Him. Whose side are we on?

That he might present it to himself a glorious church, not having spot, or wrinkle, or any such thing; but that it should be holy and without blemish.
—Ephesians 5:27

Day 43

Direction

Are you seeking direction in a time of need and want? God is your source for the answers you need. You can trust Him to lead you in the way you should go.

There is nothing like the power of the Holy Spirit helping you through it all. God sent us help in a time of need through the blood of Jesus, and He is forever present. Call upon the name of Jesus, and the Lord will answer. Some of you are waiting for financial direction, direction with a family crisis, and maybe direction in a job opportunity. Whatever the direction may be—even personal relationships—this is definitely a time for you not to lean on your own understanding (Prov. 3:5). It is time to give it to God. He is the head, and He knows everything from the beginning to the end. As a matter of fact, He knows the ending from the beginning. Is that not the best?

We have someone who cares about us and who we can truly trust because He is all-knowing. No one else can give you this kind of gift or satisfaction. God is forever pleasing. He will satisfy all of your needs. He will give you what you need when you need it. He is our perfect Keeper. There is none like Him. Look no further; He is the real deal! Go to Him! Do it today.

Trust in the Lord with all thine heart; and lean not unto thine own understanding.
—Proverbs 3:5

Day 44

The Power of Prayer

There is power in prayer! The Word says we "have not, because" we "ask not" (James 4:2). Whatever we ask for in the name of Jesus He will do (John 14:13). We have to learn how to ask the Father for what we want and what we need. We have to make sure we are lining up with the will of God. Make sure your will is His will, and God will do "exceedingly abundantly above all" you can "ask or think" (Eph. 3:20). The Word also promises, "Seek, and you will find" (Matt. 7:7, NKJV). Keep in mind that as you seek Him, He will deliver you. Find your way to receiving deliverance so you may be free from all of the old way, your way, and step into God's way, His new and fresh way!

God bless you! Fear not; God is with you always!

And whatsoever ye shall ask in my name, that will I do, that the Father may be glorified in the Son.
—John 14:13

Day 45

He Has the Final Say

***R**emember who is the first, the last, and forevermore* (Rev. 1:8). We have to know more of Him—who He is, who He was, and who He will forever be.

In this time and day we have to remember who is in control and who has the final say. Our Father who is in heaven is in control of all things and everything. God is our Father, a Father who cares about all of our needs and desires. He understands what we need, and He works out what we desire. Our desires ultimately work out together with what we need, but He has the final say in everything. We have to realize what is for our good and allow Him to do what He does, how He does it. During the process we surrender to His lordship, and we line up with Him.

This is the time in our lives where we can see more of our Lord and the movement of the Holy Spirit in ways we have never seen before. We have to learn to tap into the resurrection power of the Holy Spirit and do what our Commander-in-Chief expects of us. We want to learn to allow the Holy Spirit to move in our lives. Allow the Lord to teach you ways you can let go and ways you can grow.

I am Alpha and Omega, the beginning and the ending, saith the Lord, which is, and which was, and which is to come, the Almighty.
—Revelation 1:8

Day 46

The Takeover: Part I

Reaching out to the lost is such a rewarding position to be in. God has chosen all of us to go forth, reach the lost, win souls, cast out devils, and heal the sick (Matt. 10:8; 28:19). This generation is bolder than ever, but in this generation we as the body of Christ have to become bolder in our stand. We have to stand for something.

Let's face it: we are living in a world today that does not have any conviction, nor is there any reverence for God. There is a lack of accountability. What's more, this generation is attempting to take over. We have to stand and not be afraid to do a face-off. There have been takeovers in the home, in the schools, and in our streets. How long will we as the church sit back and allow the children of this generation to stand in their rebellion and succeed? We have to take it back! We have to turn this takeover around.

We as a people have just sat back and accepted what the enemy is using our children to do. We have given the enemy an open gate to come in and take over our homes. Don't we see? Can we not see what is behind what has been happening all of this time? Mothers have become emotionally dependent on their sons, relying on them like they would on a boyfriend or spouse to keep from being lonely. Parents often relate to their children as being their best friends, showing lack of authority. Nowadays it is becoming common for parents to be divorced or separated, leaving one of the parents to work more and longer hours, leaving the child to become an adult with responsibilities. As a result, these young people end up angry and wandering around the streets looking for love. Children are walking around our society acting angry at the world, but the real anger is toward their parents, who have abandoned their parenting duties for one reason or another. As children come into the schools full of anger it causes the teachers to fear for their lives. Children need authority figures in their lives. They need that guidance. The last thing they need or want is a best friend or a companion. They need you to operate in your ordained authority. As a church, as a people, and as parents, we must recognize that our children are so lost.

If this is not your child, pray for the children you don't know. Make this your problem. It is time to ask your children questions. It does influence your children, whether they are participants or not.

There is so much going on around us. How can we keep ignoring it? It is time for us as a society to stop fearing our children. Let us wake up out of this state of denial and do something. We have to do something! It is everybody's problem!

> Train up a child in the way he should go: and when he is old, he will not depart from it.
>
> —Proverbs 22:6

Heal the sick, cleanse the lepers, raise the dead, cast out devils: freely ye have received, freely give.
—Matthew 10:8

Day 41

The Takeover: Part II

God will reveal the tactics and the strategies of the enemy if we allow Him to. We have to pray for God to give us the discernment we need to get through from day to day. We have to realize we have to make a difference in the world.

In order to do this we have to know what is going on in this world. We cannot allow ourselves to be afraid to know. A lot of the time we don't want to know because we become accountable for the things we find out.

A perfect example of this is the current state of our children and families. We cannot ignore any longer the issues that are occurring more and more every day with our children. This generation is in need of the authority that God has ordained to be in position and do the job that is at hand. We have got to be the parent, the teacher, the law of the land, the preacher, and the elders of our communities. We have got to take a stand and no longer fear young people. We have to be bold to do a face-off with the kids in this generation. God will reward you for your labor.

It is time for the church to stand up. If you have done some work concerning this generation, find ways to do more. Network; let's come together and get more of the work done. We can *take it back,* in Jesus' name.

Day 48

Holiness

God wants us to walk in holiness. We as the body of Christ are expected by God to walk in holiness and righteousness.

Some of you are finding this hard to do. I want to encourage you that God will deliver you into holiness. He will honor your desire for more of Him and less of yourself. He knows the torment you are going through. Paul said it best: "I do the things I don't want to do, and the things I ought to do I don't do. There is a war within me, yet who shall deliver me?" (Rom. 7:15–25, author's paraphrase). God Almighty will deliver you and me. Don't live in a failure mentality. Don't allow the devil to lie to you and steal your hope. God can and He will deliver you. Nothing is too hard for God—no bad habit, no lust, no fear, no mistrust; nothing is too hard for God.

He is in control. Surrender today and allow Him to do what He does best. He parted the Red Sea for the Israelites, and He will do the same for you. We win! Trust and believe that we win. There is no greater love than what our Father in heaven has for us. Stand strong, and don't give up. *Fight, and fight hard!* How do I fight? you ask. Keep seeking the kingdom and His righteousness, and "all...things shall be added unto you" (Matt. 6:33). Seek Him and His righteousness. Keep seeking to be right with God. Keep touching the hem of His garment. Reach out to Him. He is here for you, in Jesus' name. Amen!

Day 49

Prayer Changes Things: Part I

We must exercise our right to pray. God gave us the gift of prayer. Prayer is a form of communion with God, and it is also a weapon. Prayer is a weapon against the enemy.

The Bible says that as the Lord was speaking to Peter He told him:

> I will give unto thee the keys of the kingdom of heaven: and whatsoever thou shalt bind on earth shall be bound in heaven: and whatsoever thou shalt loose on earth shall be loosed in heaven.
>
> —Matthew 16:19

The Lord right then and there gave Peter the power of prayer and declaration. It is also known to be the authority against the enemy. The keys Jesus gave him are the authority against the enemy and all of his tactics. It is also the authority to decree and declare. The Lord gave Peter—as He has given us—the authority to speak a thing into existence and to move a thing out of the way.

It is time for your prayer life to increase. Some of you wait until something goes wrong, and then you pray, but God is saying, "Now is the time to pray, before the enemy attacks." You have to get up and claim your territory. You have to seek God's face for direction to prevent any confusion. Prevention is the key. You have to build up in prayer so all your gates are closed, and the enemy won't be able to come in. Build a gate around your children, your home, your marriage, your job, your finances, your purpose, and especially your spiritual life, and protect yourself now. If you wait until something happens you are not in protecting mode; you are now in the fixing mode. Stop the devil ahead of time. Watch his movements so that you can be ready to stab him in the back with your sword, the Word of God.

Now is your time to face your fears, stop being lazy, and come out of pridefulness. It is time to pray!

He has given us—the authority to speak a thing into existence and to move a thing out of the way.

Day 50

Prayer Changes Things: Part II

When we pray it changes things. It can scatter the demons assigned to destroy us, and it can bring heaven down to us. There is power in prayer. We can break the chains of the enemy, or we can cause angels to dance in our midst.

God is in control, yet He gave us power through the blood of Jesus Christ to pull down strongholds and loose the will of God. He has given us the authority to bind and loose (Matt. 10:1). We "can do all things through Christ" Jesus, who strengthens us (Phil. 4:13). Our goal should be to rise up early and take out every plot that had been planned against the church, our lives, our families, our finances, our communities, and our nation. We have to see ourselves as warriors and kingdom-builders. Kingdom-builders have to be bold. Don't allow fear to be your portion. God gave us the inheritance to be bold in Him. We are overcomers, ambassadors, and soldiers for God.

It is time to see. Ask God to open your eyes to see. You must allow yourself to get to know God and the power of prayer. If you feel like you don't know what to say, just come before Him and speak through your heart, and I believe the Holy Spirit will guide you the rest of the way. He is our help, and He will guide us in prayer. The Lord will train you and expand you.

You have no excuse. It is time to pick up the gift of prayer. Your prayers will make a difference.

~Day 51~

Our Help Comes from the Lord

In times like these we as the body of Christ tend to want to run to a comfortable shelter, a place that will cool down the heat. Although we are "pressed on every side" (NIV), we are coming out "as gold" (2 Cor. 4:8; Job 23:10). We have to maintain our positions. We cannot run to the arms of any other; we have to run straight into the arms of God (Ps. 121). We have to remember where our help comes from. He is in our presence. Even though we may feel alone during our times of trial, He is forever present. Hold on to the personal promises He has made to you and His Word. Fight with all you've got and request more of Him. He won't let you down. Whatever you do, *don't quit,* no matter how hot the fire gets. Allow God to mold you into greatness.

We are troubled on every side, yet not distressed; we are perplexed, but not in despair.
~2 Corinthians 4:8

Day 52

Live Free of Fornication

The Lord recently revealed to me just how busy the devil is in the church, something I had noticed years ago as a young woman. My Bible says He is coming back for a bride without "spot, or wrinkle" (Eph. 5:27). My Bible also says our God has a problem with premarital sex, also known as fornicating (Gal. 5:19–20). Adultery, masturbating, and homosexuality are most important on His list of don'ts (1 Cor. 6:9). I once asked a pastor the question, Do you believe sex will ever come out of the church? He then said to me, "No," and this really saddened me. Are we so very far from the love of God that we love what our body yearns for more than we love Him? Are we more in love with the desires of our flesh than we are with God? Are we as a body enslaved to parts of our body more than we are to God? The Bible says we become a slave to whatever we give our body parts to, whether a thing or person (John 8:34; Rom. 6:13–14). We have got to get it together, people in the body of Christ! We have to learn discipline.

We have to believe we can live a life of holiness for God, the life He designed for us. We cannot allow the devil to magnify sex. We cannot allow him to antagonize us anymore. All have been tempted in this area. This is the devil's field of enjoyment. We as a church make it easy for him. We have to walk our walk with a made-up mind, not giving in to the temptation that comes to enter our senses. We have to block our gates: our ear gate, our eye gate, our mouth, hands, feet (where we go), and our loins.

We have to watch what we watch on TV and what we listen to. We have to watch out for where we walk and what we eat. Stop watching pornography, stop touching yourself, and if you are involved with someone who does not understand your walk, you have to let them go. Put away everything and all things that could lure you and seduce you into the bed of the enemy. *Don't sleep with the devil and his demons!* Stop entertaining the attacks in our dreams of the sexual night demons called the incubus and succubus. Believe God to heal you from these desires. There is nothing too hard for God.

We can say no to the enemy. The Bible says, "Resist the devil, and he will flee from you" (James 4:7). God can and He will bring you through this, for it is His perfect will for your life to live in holiness. Let us as a church break the chains that have bound the church for years!

That he might present it to himself a glorious church, not having spot, or wrinkle, or any such thing; but that it should be holy and without blemish.
—Ephesians 5:27

Day 53

Moving Forward and Upward

It is very important to keep your eyes on the prize. In order to win you must keep fighting. You must stay in the race. We have to stand our ground against all the odds. We have to summon the devil and let him know his time is up. The game is over for him. You know from the promises of God that the devil is defeated, so no matter what lie he throws your way, be determined to stand on the Word of the Lord. Your stand, along with constant prayer and praise to the King of kings, will destroy the enemy's camp.

Disciplining yourself to do this daily will only move you forward out of your situation and upward in the spirit. You have to know there is nowhere else to go but up when you apply these principles to your life. God will elevate you in your authority and in revelation. Trust God all the way. Allow the Holy Spirit to teach you and guide you. Remember who has the final say.

> Brethren, I count not myself to have apprehended: but this one thing I do, forgetting those things which are behind, and reaching forth unto those things which are before, I press toward the mark for the prize of the high calling of God in Christ Jesus.
>
> —Philippians 3:13–14

~Day 54~

New Thing

God is doing a *new thing!* Let us come into agreement and understanding of what God wants through us and wants to do for us.

It is now time for us to claim the victory over every stronghold we have been wrestling with. This is now the time to be released, restored, and recompensed. God is ready to do a new thing in your life. It is now time to come out from your own understanding and allow God to do some dumbfounding miracles in your life. It is now time! God is saying the time is now!

We have to line up with His time. Ask God to reveal to you your responsibility in getting into position for the outpour. Expect the abundance of God. He knows all you have need of, and He is the supplier of all of our needs. He will not withhold *any* good thing from you (Ps. 84:11). This is the time your enemies will be scattered. Raise Him up in this new season, and may your enemies truly be scattered, in Jesus' name!

For the LORD God is a sun and shield:
the LORD will give grace and glory:
no good thing will he withhold
from them that walk uprightly.
~Psalm 84:11

Day 55

Christlike: Part I

As we go on in our daily lives we have to remember what life is all about. What is the vision of God for the body of Christ? God's vision is for every member of the body of Christ to be walking in unbroken fellowship with Him every day so that they can experience the fullness of His plan and power in their lives. We can only do this when we have a deep knowledge of and relationship with our Lord.

God sent Jesus Christ to Earth not only for Him to bear our sins but also to serve as an example to us of how to live. Yes, He died for us to be free—thank God for His grace and mercy—and with His resurrection we have gained power. Jesus has done a lot for us and continues to do so daily as He stands in the gap for us, interceding on our behalf (Rom. 8:34). We have to look at His life as an example of how to live our lives: trusting in God, being obedient, walking in boldness, and walking in authority. He is the total example of holiness, peace, and love. He had balance and was able to walk in all of this at the same time.

We as the body of Christ need to walk in this balance. There is yet much division, judging, and criticizing going on in today's church. We have gone away from the foundation of Jesus Christ. We have gone ahead of God. We have yearned for the gifts, and our hearts are full of unforgiveness and are hard toward our brethren.

We should be unified and happy when we see the work of the Lord. We should be rejoicing over the possibility of souls being saved. This is the work of Jesus Christ.

Yes, "gifts and calling[s]...are without repentance," and we should allow God to do a work in our hearts and our spirit

(Rom. 11:29). We need to ask Him, just like David, to renew us and to create in us a clean heart (Ps. 51:10). The Bible speaks of how there were people who said to Him, "I have done this and I did that, all in Your name." God, our Father, said to them back, "I never knew you" (Matt. 7:23, see vv. 15–23).

We get to know Him each and every day by giving Him our lives; acknowledging His Son, Jesus Christ; and by walking in His example. We must do this God's way. He will never conform to our way. He is the truth, our Creator, the Creator of all things, and He is in control. We have to learn how to line up with His will, just like Jesus did. Even when Jesus struggled in Gethsemane and He asked if "this cup" could "pass away from" Him, He said, "Not my will, but your will" (Matt. 26:42, author's paraphrase). He had been reminded of His purpose and that He was to carry out His mission at His Commander's command. He was obedient unto death. What a great example!

Are we ready for this type of persecution? Are we as the body of Christ ready and willing to die for the gospel? We all make up this wonderful, beautiful body. We all have to take responsibility and do our part and then some. We have to share the vision of unity and teamwork Christ displayed Himself as He walked this earth. It is time to forgive and forget. Walk in love and wisdom.

Let us join together and build up the kingdom of God. Let's fight the devil, not one another.

We must allow God to transform our minds to be more like Christ and do the work He said we would do—even greater than Him, He said (John 14:12). Now is the time to face battles within ourselves and allow God to straighten us up, in Jesus' name.

Who is he that condemneth? It is Christ that died, yea rather, that is risen again, who is even at the right hand of God, who also maketh intercession for us.
—Romans 8:34

Day 56

Christlike: Part II

Many of us don't understand the importance of walking like Christ. Many doubters believe it doesn't take all that work to stay holy in the world today. They say we don't have to sacrifice the way they did in the biblical days. Many believe this was a way of living only in the Bible. Yet many fall short and are living way below the standard God has raised for us. There are many more who just are limited in what they believe as far as the Word of God.

The devil is the only one who has limitations. God is abundant in all things, and Jesus said we can do all things through Christ, who strengthens us (Phil. 4:13). We have to walk like Christ, think like Christ, and believe like Christ. Jesus walked this earth without a doubt about His Father. Some would argue this was because He was God in the flesh. This is true; He was God in the flesh, but even He prayed in Gethsemane for God's will to be done instead of His (Matt. 26:39). He struggled just as we do. If He struggled and persevered in righteousness, and if we know the Word promises we will do "greater works" than He did (John 14:12), then we know there is nothing we cannot do. God gave the authority to Jesus, and He then gave it to us.

We have to get to first things first. We have to learn how to be obedient unto death, as He was. We have to see ourselves as kings and ambassadors. We have been ordained by God to be overcomers and victors. We have an inheritance in the kingdom. Jesus gave a command to baptize everyone in the name of the Father, the Son, and the Holy Ghost and to make disciples, heal the sick, and cast out demons (Matt. 28:19; 10:1). Are we ready to do this? We must discipline ourselves to walk in His image. We must be obedient to the call on our lives. We must stop looking for someone else to do it and then complain about how things are done or not done. It is time to do our part as members of the body of Christ. We must intercede and stand in the gap for the weak. Everyone cannot sit on the sidelines. We must grow up and mature. Let's face it: the Word of God is the same yesterday, today, and forevermore. It is alive to those who want and choose to believe.

People! It is time to wake up and stop allowing the devil to play with your mind. It is time to move up closer. Come on! Come up a little closer. Allow God to take you higher. There is nowhere else to go but higher in Him. The harvest is plenty, "but the labourers are few" (Luke 10:2). It is time to win souls and make a difference. We have to put a stop to racism, division, and separation in the church. We have to stop playing God; there is one and only one true, living God. There was none before, and there will be none after. He is it.

We have to learn how to step out of the way and allow the Holy Spirit to move in our lives and in the church. *Stop quenching* the Holy Spirit (1 Thess. 5:19). Allow Him to move freely. The Word says it is not by might nor by power, but it is by His Spirit (Zech. 4:6). Man cannot do a thing without the Lord. Anything outside of Him will not last. Let our mind stay fixed on Him and read the Word. Be more like Christ, and spread the Word. This is our duty. He did it, and so can *you!*

Don't forget to do everything in love, in Jesus' name!

I can do all things through Christ which strengtheneth me.
—Philippians 4:13

Day 51

Calling All Backsliders!

Calling all backsliders! God is calling all the backsliders home.

If you have gone away from the Lord, listen: He said He would never leave us, nor forsake us (Heb. 13:5), yet we in the body of Christ leave Him every day by the enticement of worldly behavior or desiring worldly things and/or people. Satan's job is to get us off course and to win us away from the Lord. We have to tell the devil how it's going to be; we have got to let him know who we are and that we win. God created us, and for God we stand.

Calling all backsliders! Leave the pride at the door and humble yourselves to the call of God. He is calling you, and He wants to take you higher. Leave the past right there on the ground where it belongs. Step on it as you take the right step toward God, as He takes you higher in Him. Now is your time! God is calling all the backsliders home. He's calling you! He is waiting on you.

> Trust in the Lord...and lean not on your... understanding; In all your ways acknowledge Him, and He shall direct your paths.
>
> —Proverbs 3:5–6, NKJV

It doesn't matter what anybody says; this is your time. Don't worry about the church folks, your relatives, or your coworkers. Take this step toward your destiny. *Now* is your time! Repent now!

I pray for your strength to be renewed and that you will return to your first love. I pray for every one of you to be healed from hurt and pain, in Jesus' name. I pray that humility will be your portion today, and it will lead you to repent. In Jesus' name, amen.

Let your conversation be without covetousness; and be content with such things as ye have: for he hath said, I will never leave thee, nor forsake thee.
—Hebrews 13:5

~Day 58~

Don't Sell Yourself Short

Remember the price on your life. Remember what God gave up for you. Remember the price that was paid for you. You were bought with a high price, a price higher than even you could afford.

The Lord gave His own life for you to be set free, and who the Son has set free is "free indeed" (John 8:36). Jesus gave His life for you. What a price to pay. Who do you know who would take the blame, take your sin, get beat up—and that is saying it lightly—hang on a cross, then die, and be buried for you? Nobody but Jesus! He is the only one. When you think of making a decision with your body or your mind, make sure you consider the price on your life. The stakes are a lot higher, so don't sell yourself short. Don't bow down to anything false. Remember who you are through the blood of Jesus.

Not only is what has been placed inside of you of value, but your outside is even more valuable. God had to do work to make the vessel that carries the treasure that is within. All of your parts are of value. Don't allow the enemy to make you believe that one can go without the other. All is of a great price. Tell the devil he cannot have what has already been purchased; he cannot afford it!

If the Son therefore shall make you free, ye shall be free indeed.
~John 8:36

⊶Day 59⊷

Look What the Lord Has Done!

God is doing a work in your life! If you are reading this today you must understand divine appointment. It is not by chance that you picked up this book. The time is now for your faith to increase. The time is now for you to believe. The promises of God are at hand. God is doing a perfecting in you that will increase your faith and belief that He will do just what He said He would do (Phil. 1:6).

This is your time of deliverance into your destiny. God is preparing you to succeed and not fail. He is doing a work in you that will catapult you right into your promise. Don't allow the devil to deceive you any longer. Get right where God has ordained you to fit in. This is your time, and this is the hour of increase and expansion. Don't allow fear of change and the unknown hinder your time of growth and blessing. This is the time for your miracle to come to pass. The wait is over! This is the time of the harvest.

Receive your blessing from the Lord today. The time is now, in Jesus' name!

Being confident of this very thing, that he which hath begun a good work in you will perform it until the day of Jesus Christ.
—Philippians 1:6

Day 60

Overcoming the Spirit of Fear

The devil has released a spirit of fear in the atmosphere, and we have to take a stand against it and say, "Devil, you are a liar." We have to see the enemy's strategy in placing fear over us to take our focus off of him as the manipulator. We have to believe the Word of God and stand on it.

When the Word says, "God has not given us a spirit of fear, but of power and of love and of a sound mind" (2 Tim. 1:7, NKJV), we have to understand these words have meaning, and they are taking a bold stand against the enemy's plan to distract us from what is really going on. The devil wants to overthrow us. He wants us to be distracted from the war against him. There is no room for us to be distracted by who our president is when there is a takeover attempting to be done by the homosexual agenda. There is no time to be nervous about the economy, especially as believers, for whom God is our Source, when the spirit of Molech wants to keep murdering our babies. We as a church must take a stand against the spirit of fear. We have to continue to build our faith by reading the Word of God and walking boldly. We have to stand for righteousness.

Now is your time to say *no* to the enemy! God bless each and every one of you, in Jesus' name.

Now is your time to say no to the enemy!

Day 61

Take Time Out

With all you do, know that your labor is not in vain (1 Cor. 15:58). Remember, there is always time for rest. When we rest, we trust. Believe God to take care of what you can't. He will fill in the blanks. There is no way you can be everywhere at every time. Take time to rest, like the farmers. After they have toiled and sowed, they have a time of wait. Waiting is resting and trusting in the work you have done. For believers it means believing the work you have done is pleasing to the Lord and waiting for recompense. You are in waiting for your harvest; you are waiting for your hundredfold.

With every good work, know when to rest. All of the great pioneers knew that they needed to rest, and it always worked for them. Even Jesus knew when to rest (Matt. 8:23–27). David learned very quickly how the enemy wants to wear you out. He loves to come in when you are tired. He wants you to be torn down and tired out, which is why God requires us to get the rest we need (Gen. 2:2).

In your time of rest, God will honor your faithfulness. He will make everything plain for you. You won't miss a thing. Rest for the Lord, in the name of Jesus. It will do your body, mind, and soul some good. When the time is up, get back up and do it all over again with all diligence, for He is the rewarder of them that diligently seek Him (Heb. 11:6).

Day 62
A Taste

The other day I went to Sam's Club, and I ran across an older woman who was preparing breakfast biscuits and coffee. You know how they prepare samples for you to test while you are shopping. The smell is to seduce you into tasting the products, and then hopefully you will buy. Well, as we were approaching this lady's table I noticed a big wall of sorts in front of her. It was a spiritual wall, black and thick. I then said hello to her and asked, "How are you?" She wanted to pretend that we were not there so that she did not have to fix our biscuits. I started to notice another group coming up to the station wanting the same thing, a taste. As we waited for her to prepare the biscuit for us, very begrudgingly I might add, I stirred up a conversation with her. This woman had nothing to give God thanks for. She complained about her job, and she complained about her working on that day. She had not one good thing to say, and her attitude made it less tempting to try anything she had prepared. Let's just say we didn't want to taste anything she had fixed.

How can we, in a time like this, have nothing good to say? Take a look over your life. I am sure most of you can find something God has done for you yesterday and today. If you woke up this morning, that means God has given you another opportunity to be blessed. If you can get yourself dressed, you are blessed. If you are able to stand, to walk, to bend, to jump, to speak, to see, my God, you are blessed. Give God thanks for something today. Come out of what you don't have and step into what God has blessed you with today. This is the day that the Lord has made, so *you* should rejoice and be glad in it.

After realizing the woman wasn't going to budge, we all then decided to leave her table—without a taste and without purchasing a thing. I, in turn, said to her, "God bless you," and walked away feeling even more thankful that I can see all that He has done for me. Come and "taste and see that the LORD is good" (Ps. 34:8). God bless you, in Jesus' name.

O taste and see that the LORD is good: blessed is the man that trusteth in him.
—Psalm 34:8

Day 63

Waiting

We have entered into a new season and a new level. The Lord is raising up the body of Christ. We are taking over! Sound the alarm and let the world know the time has come for the body of Christ, the true believers, to take it all back! We are taking over the media, the music industry, the movie industry, and television. We are taking it over! We say thanks to the world, and now it is our turn. The wealth of the wicked is stored up for the righteous (Prov. 13:22). We have waited for this time. It's time to celebrate who you are as you wait on your orders.

God has been and is continuing to pour into His people the wisdom, the strength, and the strategy against our enemies for such a time as this. We are more than equipped! God says some of us are ready now and are in position. There is no time for intimidation. We must go forth as the Lord leads and do His will. He has already stirred up this generation, who is radical for Him and ready to please. They are creative, gifted, and on fire for God. Keep them in prayer. As we pray, continue to pray for the young, the old, and for all races to follow the will of God.

It is time! We have been waiting to see a move of God on this magnitude, and now is the time! We have waited, and even as we continue to wait allow Him to do the work in you so that you, too, can be ready to be used "on earth as it is in heaven" (Matt. 6:10, NKJV).

The Lord has given us dominion over the earth. Remember, we are children of the King. He is the King of all kings. There were none before Him, and there will never be any after Him. He is the only true and living God.

Day 64

God Is in Control

Regardless of what people think or want to believe, God is in control. No matter what laws may pass under the church's nose God is in control. No matter what you may be going through God is in control. No matter what the doctor is saying God is in control. *No matter what* the enemy *is saying*, what lies he is telling, *God is still in control, and He has the final say.* Believe the report of the Lord and stand your ground no matter what. The Word of God is your truth. Your children are saved, healed, and delivered. Your husband/wife is delivered. God has the final say! And He is in *control.*

> See, it is I who created the blacksmith who fans the coals into flame and forges a weapon fit for its work. And it is I who have created the destroyer to wreak havoc.
>
> —Isaiah 54:16, NIV

Believe the report of the Lord and stand your ground no matter what.

Day 65

Transitioning into Positioning

Hey, don't sweat the small stuff! Remember who is in control.

God, your Father, predestined you before you were even born. This is a big deal! He knows you better than you know yourself. He chose you first. He had a plan for you before your mother even thought of you. This plan He spoke over you started as a word, and He said that His Word will not return to Him void (Isa. 55:11). Isn't this great news?

Now, what does this mean to you? What are you supposed to do with this information at this point? Surrender! Surrender all to Him. Give it up! You cannot not win without Him. To succeed and enter into the greatness He has planned for you, you must let go and let God. He has got to do it; He made the blueprint for your life. He knows the game and the players involved. You cannot do it any better. He said eyes have "not seen, nor ear heard" the plans He has for you (1 Cor. 2:9, NKJV). Well, I don't know about you, but this says a whole lot to me. It means I need to sit my butt down and let Him take charge. He can do it best.

While we allow Him to put the pieces all together, He wants us to seek Him. Be active in our wait. While we wait, He wants us to trust Him. The disciples had no idea what they were going to be doing, and most of the time they had no idea where they were going, but they surrendered all and followed the anointing. They surrendered to the move of God to be led by Jesus Christ, who received His orders from our Father God Almighty. We have to do the same. To achieve we must assume the position of follower of Christ. Follow His example. Remember, His track record was success.

God has called us to be successful and prosperous in all things according to His purpose for our lives. Stand in the position of being led by the Lord.

So shall my word be that goeth forth out of my mouth: it shall not return unto me void, but it shall accomplish that which I please, and it shall prosper in the thing whereto I sent it.
—Isaiah 55:11

Day 66

Tell Frustration to Go!

This is the day the LORD has made. We will rejoice and be glad in it.

—PSALM 118:24, NKJV

R*emember, God is your source of strength*. Don't allow the devil to steal any of your time. Ask the Lord for peace that passes "all understanding" (Phil. 4:7). The enemy's job is to steal, and this is what he sets out to do (John 10:10).

I know in the course of your day things can get on your nerves. Yes! I am talking to God's people, the believers. Now, don't get all religious on me; we are not in church. Some of you know when you are not in church it is a different face that you put on. We have to learn to keep on Jesus all the time. We cannot put Him on, on Sunday and take Him off from Monday—Saturday. We like to put Him on going to church and take Him off when we are not in church. For Sunday service, Bible Tuesday, or Wednesday, and Friday, put Him on. No, this is not what He is expecting from us. The Lord wants us to represent Him at all times.

Look, I know this is challenging. I have been there, and I have had to count to one hundred. I know people will try you. I know about road rage. I get it. Yet, even at these times we have to hold it down. We have to take the bigger step. We must seek Him for His strength. The funny part about this is that most of the time we are fussing at each other. The cashier, the worker at the fast food joint, our coworkers—more than likely they are saved sons and daughters of Christ. Somebody has to stand up. Some believers are more mature, or should be, and therefore should be an example of self-control (Gal. 5:22–23). We must exercise maturity in Jesus' name. We can take authority over frustration in Jesus' name. We don't have to have our emotions played with any longer. If there is a place or person that can just pull the old out of you, find a solution from the Lord in what you need to do. You are a new creature (2 Cor. 5:17)! War out, or get out!

I pray against the spirit of frustration that you all will be free to walk in peace. This is what God has promised us. We can no longer enjoy what the flesh wants, and that is to stand in frustration. We must learn self-control. Maybe this is the way you have been taught, but God can retrain you. He can give you what you need for the day. Allow Him to give you your portion. Start now in Jesus' name. I believe you will have much success in all the days to come.

You will notice a change, like that you are now picking your battles. Some things are just not worth it. Let go and let God. I have seen Him move right in and deal with the situation. We don't have anything to prove. He is the Vindicator. He will fight for you. Stand your ground in His name. Other than that, what is it all about? You win every time with Him in it. God bless you.

And the peace of God, which passeth all understanding, shall keep your hearts and minds through Christ Jesus.
—Philippians 4:7

Day 67

Reclaiming Our Youth

We have summoned the enemy to battle! We are taking back our youth! The time is now! No more playing around, fighting one day, getting tired, and putting it down. We are picking it back up, and we are staying there until we see a change. No longer will believers be afraid of their children. No longer will believers be afraid of those demons attacking our youth. No longer will we stand by and just say, "That's how their daddy was/is," or, "That's how their mother was/is." No more! They are going to be more like Christ.

We don't have to fear their reaction or even fear what we may do to them. We have to remember we are fighting a spirit that wants to take over and destroy our youth (Eph. 6:12). We have to take a stand. *Really!* We must fight with all we've got.

God wants to use these young people for His kingdom. If they have talent they can make use of it for God's kingdom. Their gifts and talents were given to them for just that. Success does not always mean giving it to the world. We can be in the world but not of the world (John 17:15–16). When God opens the doors for us to go into the marketplace, He is expecting us to be light and to win souls by being examples, not to be taken over by the world.

Wake up! We have to realize the media—music, television, the movies, social media (Facebook, Snapchat, Twitter, Instagram)—are taking our children. They have been hypnotized and seduced into a trance. If this is not your kid or you don't know anyone like this, read the newspaper, go around the corner, talk to a neighbor.

Investigate! This is really going on. Some of these avenues may look innocent, but we need to look with the eyes of Christ. Ask God to increase your vision.

We can, and we will do this. We have to. Our children are really in need and want some guidance. Believe it or not, they really do want it from you. Yet we have to make sure our house, our temple, is in order. They want the truth, and nothing but the truth. Ask God for the help and the strategy you need to win our youth back in your region. We are going to do this. They are our end-time warriors, and they cannot see. We have to fight for them until they are strong enough to hold it down on their own (Josh. 1:14–15). Pray and believe God for the strength to fight.

For we wrestle not against flesh and blood, but against principalities, against powers, against the rulers of the darkness of this world, against spiritual wickedness in high places.
—Ephesians 6:12

Day 68

Trust in the Lord

Every day when we look in the mirror, what do we see? Oftentimes we see something we wish wasn't there, and we often want to fix it.

I remember before I was walking with Christ I would sometimes see darkness, a hardness of some sort, when I looked at myself in the mirror. Most of the time I would ignore it and go on with the day, claiming it was age. Many times I would choose to ignore it with something self-destructing to camouflage what I had seen. When we are not living in the will of God it will take a toll on us. We may not notice it at first, but it will catch up to us. You see, the beauty of God is in those who serve God. Living in the flesh brings forth death, and living for God brings forth life (Rom. 6:23). When I was living in the flesh what I saw in the mirror was death. Although we are aging and we are getting older every day, looking like death was not God's plan. We are glorifying God when we are living for Him and revealing His beauty in us.

When I turned my life over to the Lord again by saying the sinner's prayer and then surrendering to Him, did I see my countenance change. I started seeing the glory of God shining through the darkness. Death was leaving, and life was coming through. I promise you, after seeking the Lord on a regular basis and giving my life to Him He led me back to the mirror. He told me to look at myself. That was the day I knew I was in my process of transformation and I had been changed. I saw a beauty in me that I had never seen before. It was the beauty of the Lord. I have to say, I did not recognize myself. I had been changed, praise God.

This was only the beginning. God still had a work to do, but at that point what He allowed me to see had changed me completely. I was determined to stand still and watch the salvation of the Lord (Exod. 14:14). The work He had done with His own hands no man could take credit for. No doctor, no makeup, no stylist, no gym, no man could take credit for what God had done. Like the Word says, I was beginning to see the manifestation of His promise that He will complete the *good* work He had started in me, and I was looking for more (Phil. 1:6). Now I pray, "From the inside out and from the outside in, complete me, Lord."

Trust the Lord to transform you. He will do a better job than we can do ourselves through our own effort, I assure you.

Being confident of this very thing, that he which hath begun a good work in you will perform it until the day of Jesus Christ.
—Philippians 1:6

Day 69

Love Yourself

This morning I felt the Lord wanted me to write about loving yourself. God wants us to lay down our lives, but if we don't love ourselves, how can we lay our lives down in love for someone else (Luke 9:23)?

Most of the time we as God's children feel unworthy, or our aim is to please other people anyway. It is interesting how we tend to put ourselves on the back burner. We as a society in the kingdom of God walk around defeated. But God is training us to love ourselves. Jesus gave His life in boldness and in confidence. When Jesus was praying for the cup to pass by Him, God gave Him enough strength to go up on that cross in full confidence of who He is and what honor it was to be created and chosen for such a call (Matt. 26:39). We too must have this same mind that was in Christ. We must learn to love ourselves as our Father loves us. How can we ever really know His love for us if we are walking around in self-hate and self-condemnation? He wants us to walk in freedom and in truth. There is no condemnation in Him, so there should be none in us (Rom. 8:1). Allow Him to show you your worth. Now is the time to be free, for who the Son has set free is free indeed (John 8:36).

Now, there may be some of us that think too highly of ourselves. Most of the time this too is a camouflage of some sort. God will give the balance you need to walk in spirit and in truth. He loves the humble, but we can tend to make humility a "woe is me" thing. God will give you balance.

It is time to believe the report of the Lord about who you are. You are a child of the most high God (Ps. 82:6). You are the creation of God. He created you in His image (Gen. 1:27).

Remember this, think on this, and allow the Lord to transform you. Cast out those lying demons. Tell the devil he is a liar. Let those demons know you will not settle for less any longer. You will lay down your life in confidence, not in defeat. You are the winner. Many will be set free from your testimony. God will use your life for you to do great exploits. You are worthy, and you are worth loving. God loves you, and He knows you love Him. Now love yourself, in Jesus' name.

And he said to them all, If any man will come after me, let him deny himself, and take up his cross daily, and follow me.
—Luke 9:23

Day 10

What a Mighty God We Serve

Thank You, Father, for not being like man.

God is so faithful, and yet we still don't understand His sovereignty. He is forgiving, and He is diligent in perfecting what He has created.

People, on the other hand, have a problem with giving up, giving up on life and people. We have struggled with this as a people, as a generation, from generation to generation. From races and customs we have struggled, yet through it all God has made a way of escape (1 Cor. 10:13). Some have made it past these struggles, and some may not have in the years past. Regardless of man's track record in this area, we have to be determined not to give up on God and His commandments or on others. We cannot walk away from His power or His people and expect to remain blessed. We are accountable for what we do know, because His faithfulness to us is evident in all of creation (Rom. 1:20). We understand God to have a way of increase and a way of making it better for the next generation, and we have to take the advantages God has laid up for us.

Some of you think if you love your pastor very much and you love how he preaches and handles the church, it is OK to not love the flock he is leading. When you stand for the pastor, you stand for the vision he has for the church, which should be loving one another, helping one another, and submitting to one another. This is true love for the leader. We should see God as this; we should see God as our Creator and our Leader. We should love what He loves and hate what He hates. We should do and be all He is expecting from us. This is kingdom vision "on earth as it is in heaven" (Matt. 6:10, NKJV). "A house...divided" will not last, so let Him start with yours (Mark 3:25).

We have all the resources we need to move past our struggles and into the will of the Lord. We cannot blame the people who have hurt us, wounded us, or rejected us for our struggles. We have to choose to forgive and walk in love. There are a lot of God's people battling with sickness and infirmities because of unforgiveness and because they have given up. Get back up and take your stand against the lies of the devil. He wants you to believe you are alone and that no one loves you or even likes you. Who cares who likes you? God *loves* you and has people waiting for you (John 3:16). Allow Him to heal your heart so He can build relationships of love surrounding you. The truth is, God "will never leave you nor forsake you" (Heb. 13:5) and knows exactly what you need and who you need. Wake up out of the slumber, and take back your life. The plans God has for you are not determined by what someone has done or said to you. His plans for your life will continue to come to pass as long as you don't give up on God and all He stands for. He has already equipped you to prosper!

This is an hour of repenting. God is calling us forth to repent and turn from our wicked ways, thoughts, and actions. Then He will heal our land, our households, and our broken hearts (2 Chron. 7:14).

> In the past God overlooked such ignorance, but now he commands all people everywhere to repent.
>
> —Acts 17:30, NIV

We cannot walk away from His power or His people and expect to remain blessed.

~ Day 71 ~

The Captain of the Ship

God's Word will *never* change, but it can change everything (Mal. 3:6). When we read the Word, we study to show ourselves "approved" (2 Tim. 2:15). We begin to transform in understanding who our God really is. We began to see the Holy Spirit as our friend, a comforter, and our help (John 14:16). We start to see the love of Christ and how God, Christ, and the Holy Spirit are all *one.*

We also begin to get the understanding that God is in control. He is the Captain of this ship. He is running everything. He created the coals and the fire (Isa. 54:16). He has His hands on top of it all. Nothing gets by Him. He knows all and He sees all. As we dive deeper into the Word our minds begin to transform as we start to understand and get the revelation that our Father will never change to adapt to our ways. He will only change you to adapt to His ways, His precepts, and His statutes.

What I love about my Daddy is He is loving and powerful. He is powerful in loving. If we learn to trust Him we will see the purposes and plans in His Word. Are we ready to give up and give in to Him?

Reading the Word allows us to begin to know His voice. He said His sheep would "know His voice" (John 10:4). Are we truly ready to get the full 411 on who it is we serve?

Jesus is the Way, the Truth, and the Light (John 14:6). We must go through Him to get to the Father. Give your life to Him today. If you have, make your mind up today to be transformed in all He has for you. If you feel like you are a good person already, humble yourself and be better. God can make us better. God bless you, and remember, God will make it plain to you if you are willing to open up to Him.

And I will pray the Father, and he shall give you another Comforter, that he may abide with you for ever.
—John 14:16

Day 72

The Secret Is...It's The Enemy

I was at my favorite store yesterday, Ikea. If you follow me you on Twitter you are aware I frequent there quite a bit. (I love it!) As I was sitting there in the restaurant area a very nice gentlemen sat next to me. He seemed very ambitious and excited about life. He started a conversation with me, which went along with the normal meet, greet, and network thing. He proceeded to tell me he was an interior designer, which is something I had gone to college for myself. We began to talk even more, me listening more than talking, which I have grown to do. Thank God for His changing hands. He then asked me what I did for a living. I told him briefly about my salvation, the ministries, my book *Born into Sin, Transformed into Destiny*, and just life with Christ.

You see, I knew this wasn't by chance. I knew this was a God thing. He told me he was saved and he had an encounter with the Lord. He remembered the year and what he was going through at the time. It was exciting to hear what he was saying, but my discernment was telling me something different. I could discern confusion, and I just saw a shadow in front of him, like a blockage of some sort. I listened, was patient, and followed the flow of the Holy Spirit. Then there it came. He spoke about making things happen through your thoughts. New Age witchcraft was revealed.

The marketing strategy of the enemy is to manipulate the thoughts of the people—and God's people—to believe we can take control over our own lives, that we don't need God. This is a lie. How can we not need God when He is in control of everything? He created the coal and the fire (Isa. 54:16). We need Him for everything. The devil's job is to misinform people, like he tried to do with Jesus after His forty-day fast. The forces of the enemy try to market these things based on biblical facts, just like Satan did with Eve and with Jesus, but with Jesus he failed. Those who are not studying themselves "approved" will fall into this trap (2 Tim. 2:15), but God "is able to keep... [us] from falling" if we allow Him to (Jude 1:24).

This gentleman told me he believed this was the strategy that was going to help him launch his business. I then said to him, as led by the Holy Spirit, "The Word says God will do exceedingly and abundantly above *all* we ask or *think*." (See Ephesians 3:20.) I told him that even as hard as he thinks, God has got something even better than that—and it will be everlasting. When God opens a door, "no man can shut it" (Rev. 3:8), but if he relies on his thoughts, which is in operation with Satan, along with his fleshly desires, any success he gains will not last. Doors will shut.

God is in control! How many know God says, "My thoughts are not your thoughts, neither are your ways my ways" (Isa. 55:8). Our Father also says what we do in the secret place He will reward us openly, and everything done in the dark will be revealed (Matt. 6:1–4). God has blessed you to live in prosperity in Him (3 John 2). Please read your Bible. It is your sword in war and the key to living in freedom. Don't allow the enemy to tempt you.

The young man and I exchanged cards, and I encouraged him to hang on and to keep his focus on the Lord. I blessed him in Jesus' name and left to pick up my son. God got the glory, praise God. Truth was revealed, and the devil was brought to open shame. Amen. Be encouraged, every one of you, in Jesus' name.

The marketing strategy of the enemy is to manipulate the thoughts of the people

Day 13

How Are You Feeling?

I want to tell you to *pay no attention to your feelings.* Why? They will get you into trouble. Most times, if we pay attention to them they will tell us, "It is too much. I can't take it anymore. I should be doing more. My feelings are hurt, etc." What do we do with those feelings? We take them to our Father. We lay them out before Him, and we allow Him to make sense of them. As we continue to do this we build up and we mature. At some point you will grow and realize that these are feelings and realign your focus and begin to live on purpose, not on feelings.

You see, the devil knows how to push our buttons. He knows just what to use to get us off focus and off track. We have to be wise of his tactics and resist him as quickly as possible (James 4:7). The work of the enemy is to pull us out of position and cause us to doubt God is working for us and through us. We are taught in the Word to guard our heart, the gifts, and the promises of God (Prov. 4:23). As we do this, we won't allow the demons that play on our emotions to win. We have to realize we win! Yes, I'll say it again: *we win!* We cannot allow the devil to come in and take over. The Word says to not be offended, so don't allow offense to take you out of the position God has created for you (Prov. 19:11). Remember who is in control.

Now, the next time someone asks you, "How are you feeling?" You tell them, "Like a winner!" and, "I am blessed." God bless you, in Jesus' name!

Day 74

The Issachar Anointing

This is a perfect time to line up with God's timing. We must know what season we are in (1 Chron. 12:32). It is time-out for being in the dark. We must go forth with the light, the truth. Some of us are walking in denial, and we need to wake up. We are still in the same place we were last season. The thing is, as we walk in the right season we will learn what we need to learn in that season.

You see, just because a word has been prophesied over us does not mean that we are in the season to receive it. It just means we can write it down, "make it plain," and wait for that word to manifest (Hab. 2:2). We have to realize what season we are in. Are we in a season of waiting, a season of elevation, a season of maturity, a season of impartation? Or are we in a season of manifestation? We must seek His face to know where we stand. We cannot be blindsided any longer with delusions and selfish desires. Our desires have to line up with the will of God.

It is time to know the truth and walk by faith. It is time for us to be challenged. We cannot run away from the fire of God, which will make us better. We must face our fears. It is the time and the season for elevation for sure. Don't miss out on the outpour. God bless you!

And the Lord answered me, and said, Write the vision, and make it plain upon tables, that he may run that readeth it.
—Habakkuk 2:2

Day 75

We Should Not Be Ashamed

We should not be ashamed of the gospel of Jesus Christ. He became poor so we could become rich (2 Cor. 8:9). He gave His life for us so we would walk in total victory over the enemy. Yet we as the body of Christ are still living in poverty mentally. We have to rise up out of the minimum and get into kingsmanship. We are joint heirs to the kingdom of God (Rom. 8:17). We are ambassadors (2 Cor. 5:20). Why would we settle for anything less?

God is a Father of recompense. He is our rewarder, and yet we still don't believe Him to really come through for us like He said He would. We live in doubt and disbelief. We are looking every which way but to Him. He said our ways are not His ways, and our thoughts are not His thoughts (Isa. 55:8). We are different in our understanding, yet He invites us to come to His throne to become more like Him.

He wants our mind to be set on Him and for us to have the mind of Christ (Phil. 2:5). He wants us to get to know Him and to become more like Him. When we come to His throne on a regular basis we will then began to see things the way He sees things, and we will leave from Him believing in Him even more, that what He said He *would* do He *will* do. We will live with more wisdom, and our vision will be clearer. We have to understand before we miss this move that He will do it, but He is going to do it where He will get the glory. He wants man to know He is in control. He wants the world to know the God we serve. He will do it "exceedingly" and "abundantly above all" you can ever "ask or think" (Eph. 3:20). He will do it bigger than you can imagine. This is what He wants us to look for, *bigger and better!* He wants to really show us our worth to Him and how He put it all together masterfully, greater than any man could. Open your eyes so you can see. *Our view has been shifted!*

For ye know the grace of our Lord Jesus Christ, that, though he was rich, yet for your sakes he became poor, that ye through his poverty might be rich.
—2 Corinthians 8:9

Day 76

Let Your Voice Be Heard

This is the time when the voice of God's people needs to be heard. It is time to sound the alarm. This is not the time for folks to go running and hiding, hiding behind race, socioeconomic status, and segregated organizations, period. We have got to stop hiding behind man and stand up in the face of these giants in the land (Num. 13:31–33). It is the time right *now!* We cannot prolong this anymore.

We have got to become more aware of what is going on in our surroundings. We cannot afford to continue to walk in the "I didn't know" frame of mind. It is time to come out! And to shout, "We are not going to take this anymore, Satan!" We have to make him give back our land. We have to tell him to give it back hundredfold. This is the time *now!* God is raising up a remnant who will be bold, who will say and who will shout what the Lord is saying. He is raising up Moseses and Davids with the anointing that will destroy the yokes of the enemy. It is time to break the devil's back and crush his head in. Enough is enough!

Do we see what is happening? The time has come where the enemy of this land is not being sneaky anymore. These things are happening right in our faces. We are either blind and can't see, turning our heads in the other direction, or we are in agreement. We have to stop being scared, playing church and pretending we are operating in power when clearly something is off. We are not operating in the power God has ordained for us, because we have ceased to be a source of counsel in our nation. We have become the last voice the government dares to seek counsel from, unless it is for an election. We as a church should be present some way, somehow, sought after for counsel before a bill is even presented. It is as if we don't matter anymore. It's as if our voice matters not. We have to make our voices heard. We cannot allow the government, or anyone else for that matter, to water down who we are in Christ. We are ambassadors on this earth. We have been given a mandate. We have been ordained by God. Write a letter, speak to your church leaders, call your local Congressman's office, or join forces with the groups that are about kingdom building and not segregation and separation.

We need to focus more on the kingdom than anything else right now. The Word says to seek His kingdom first, and His righteousness, and "all...things shall be added unto you" (Matt. 6:33). We don't have any more time to live in the past. We have got to attack our target, and that is the devil himself. Don't allow him to distract you anymore. The time is now to fight back! Selah and shalom.

We don't have any more time to live in the past. We have got to attack our target, and that is the devil himself.

Day 77

I Am Often Reminded

As I continue to seek the Lord I am often reminded of what He has done for my life. Too frequently we may hear a sermon, and the preacher may mention a few of the things the Lord's blood has done. It may happen to slip in the sermon here and there. Most times people are ashamed to tell all that the Lord has done. I can tell you there are more people that don't know what He has truly done. Their hope has gone away, and their eyes have been shut closed by the devil's lies.

People need to hear about what the Lord has done. When you pick up my book *Born into Sin, Transformed into Destiny* you will get the truth about what the Lord has done in my life. I can tell you now, through all I have gone through it is a wonder I still have the sense to tell it. I could have truly lost my mind a long time ago. I will tell you this, it had to be the Lord who stopped the enemy from taking it, because I surely gave him the leeway to take it. I can say I have made some bad choices—very bad—and yet by the grace of God I stand to tell it all. The Lord commissioned me to write my first book because, believe it or not, I have truly gone through some horrible experiences that a child through her young adult years should not have gone through, yet by God's grace I stand to tell it.

Most of the time we want to forget what we have experienced. We may still be carrying some shame and don't want anybody to know what we went through, but God told me to shame the devil. I believe in testimony. I believe it heals the soul, and it changes lives. The Lord told me He would turn my ashes to beauty (Isa. 61:3), so why should I fear man? "If God be for" me, "who can be against" me (Rom. 8:31)? The Lord has commanded us to go out and cast out demons and heal the sick (Matt. 10:8). How can anybody see the glory of God if they cannot truly see the glorified work He has done in our lives? He has truly brought me out of a pit. I have come out, and I have risen with Christ. Now it is time for me to help set the captives free. There are many out there who don't mind sharing the full gospel of what He has done for them, so let us multiply and set the captives free.

It is time to take the shame garments off and put on your priestly garments and walk in boldness. Shame the enemy! You may not be able to tell it in a book form, like myself and many others, but how about at a given opportunity? God will and can present an opportunity for you to share the work He has done in your life. We may feel like this is not necessary, or we may be afraid of what people will think about it. Don't allow fear to stop you from giving your testimony. Believe me, you will be surprised how many others have gone through what you have gone through, and maybe even at times they may share that they have been through worse. The thing is, as you are releasing, God is getting the glory, you are being set free, and the enemy can no longer keep you in the bondage of past failures. You silence him this way. As God is lifted up, all men will be drawn unto Him (John 12:32). The woman at the well went and told the people about what Jesus had done for her, and look at all she had done (John 4:1–30). She told the testimony, and then she told the people, "You need to go see the man at the well."

Go on and tell your story and shame the devil. You will set the captives free, all in Jesus' name!

To appoint unto them that mourn in Zion, to give unto them beauty for ashes, the oil of joy for mourning, the garment of praise for the spirit of heaviness; that they might be called trees of righteousness, the planting of the LORD, that he might be glorified.
—Isaiah 61:3

~Day 78~

In Need of Guidance

God gives us the opportunity to seek Him for His guidance for the day. He wants us to involve Him in our everyday living. He said if we knock He will answer (Matt. 7:7). Whatever we have need of—wisdom, or whatever else it may be—we are to ask Him, and He will supply all we need (James 1:5). The thing is, we have to seek Him. We have to allow Him to give us the guidance we need daily. We need our Father to guide us to success. We cannot do anything without Him. Many have tried, and their successes did not last. Nothing lasts without the Father being in it, doing it, or protecting it. We must get guidance from the one who knows all, the all-knowing God Himself! He will be able to lead us around the enemy's traps and snares. He is the one who will guide you to those who He has ordained to take you to the next level in your walk with Him.

It is very important for us to surrender to the leading, the guidance of our Father God almighty, and He will deliver us to success. Enjoy your walk with Christ. He will guide you through every step of the way.

Ask, and it shall be given you; seek, and ye shall find; knock, and it shall be opened unto you.
—Matthew 7:7

Day 79

Breaking Your Silence

There is no greater satisfaction then to tear up the plans of the enemy. We can do just that by sharing our testimony.

We can literally break up the plans of the enemy by revealing his strategy to others. The enemy is a counterfeit. He often does the same thing over and over again. Believe me, he has no creativity. In other words, he often does it the same way—different place, different face. We can gain more momentum by sharing our testimony (Rev. 12:11). Most people find that revealing such truth is rewarding, and it is satisfying. We can lay it all on the line for Christ. Through our testimony we show people just how good God really is and how He truly cares for us. We can help by being transparent and not being ashamed of what God has brought us out of. We should humble ourselves and lay our lives down on the line for the gospel.

We are actually spreading the gospel with our testimony. It is called spreading the good news. We are freeing people from the spirit of fear when we share our testimony. We are keeping people from feeling alone, like they are the only one, through our testimony. We are imparting wisdom when we share our testimony. We are encouraging people when we share our testimony.

Share your testimony today. Give your life as a sacrifice unto the Lord and be used by the words of your mouth to help set the captives free and bring shame to the enemy. We can win!

Day 80

Walking on a Tightrope

When we give our lives to Christ we are immediately elevated. We are raised up in the blood of Jesus. We are on a higher level, and we rise above our enemies. We gain victory over those demons that tried so desperately to keep us from crossing on the other side of Christ's blood covenant. Now what do we do?

God gave me a vision of a man walking on a tightrope. If you look down while walking the tightrope you may start to wobble, and you are too high to fall down. You may fall down too hard and lose it all. Likewise, you cannot go up any higher without God first raising up the bar. We have to wait on God to take us higher. When the Lord showed me this vision I saw Jesus standing at the end of the rope, and the man was being coached from where He was. You may be at the beginning, but remember, you did step out there. You stepped out on faith, so now keep going; He is waiting at the end for you. You may have been creeping and sliding slowly until now, but now you are closer to the middle. You have come too far. No matter how long it took for you to get there, don't turn back now. Keep pushing. You may be past the middle. You have come a long way, baby! Keep on going. Don't look down! Keep your eyes on the prize, because you are closer than you think. The great thing about all of this is, He is waiting for us all. So no matter where you are, the only place to go is straight forward to Him on the tightrope.

Not as though I had already attained, either were already perfect: but I follow after, if that I may apprehend that for which also I am apprehended of Christ Jesus. Brethren, I count not myself to have apprehended: but this one thing I do, forgetting those things which are behind, and reaching forth unto those things which are before, I press toward the mark for the prize of the high calling of God in Christ Jesus.

—PHILIPPIANS 3:12–14

Don't look down! Keep your eyes on the prize, because you are closer than you think.

Day 81

Running into the Arms of the Wrong Person

We as people tend to become needy at some point in our lives. Like the song says, we begin to look for love from unhealthy sources. I believe this begins from birth. The Lord revealed to me that when we are born, we are born in His image, and His image is of love (Gen. 1:27). He predestined us out of love for fellowship, for worship, and to celebrate Him. When we are in our mother's womb we look for this nurturing then, and we continue this pursuit when we come out.

Think of a baby bird. That bird is hopping around, looking for the nurturing he needs to gain wisdom and knowledge, to learn the dos and don'ts, to get encouragement when he is fearful, to learn to walk confidently and in trust. The baby bird, like ourselves, is at a young age looking for what God created in him. We need this knowledge too. This is the foundation that a person is built upon.

Studies have proven that the period from in the womb to thirteen years old is the most important age of a child's life. This is the age at which they are grabbing and taking in the good or the negative. We as parents have this responsibility. If we have children, no matter if we never have a dime in our pockets and nothing to give, if we are homeless and cannot provide a shelter over our family's head, or if there is no father figure in the home or no mother, we are and will always be parents. The Word says to raise your children in the way that they "should go," and when they grow old it will never part from them (Prov. 22:6).

Love, encouragement, stability, confidence, and trust are all attributes of our Father, the most high God, who created us in His image. So where has the love gone? If you grew up looking for love in all the wrong places, or if you have known of your children growing up this way, there has been some lack, crack, or split in their foundation. Your children should always see you as a foundation of love and encouragement, as a cheerleader and confidant. Just like the bird as a little one is chasing after his mother looking for reassurance, so are our children looking to us. When the time comes for the bird to be released on his own into the world, that mother bird is then confident she has laid the foundation and has given it her all to assure the bird that he can do it. She is so confident that when the time comes for the bird to go on his own, she drops the bird over a cliff or from a tree so the bird can spread its wings and soar.

Look at our past and the present. God wants you to know there is no greater love than His, and He is your Source (John 15:13). Whatever you have lacked and lived without, guess what: you made it for such a time as this. You made it into His arms. You may not know how to receive love, and you may have been looking for it in all the wrong places, but God is here to tell you today there is no greater love than His, so receive it with open arms. No one can love you like the Father can. He will teach you the way you should go, and it is never too late. He is your foundation; He was from the very beginning. You just had to find your way home to Him.

God bless you. Please build your relationship with Him and stop running into the arms of the wrong people. God is the Way, the Truth, and the Life (John 14:6). No one can restore and replenish like He can. He wants to do it for you right now! Stop for a moment and look toward the hills, where your help comes from; it comes from the Lord (Ps. 121:1–2). Be still and know that He is God.

Day 82

Life Changes

Living a life for Christ can cause you to see many changes in life. You can count on a shifting to take place. You see, when we are living on our own we can tend to pick up people, places, and habits that simply don't match up to God's perfect plan for our lives. We don't realize at these moments in life that we are truly settling for minimum. We tend to settle for less than God's best for us, even though the Bible says God will do "exceedingly" and "abundantly" above all you can ask or think (Eph. 3:20).

This got me thinking, since the Lord has started taking me through a transformation, did I truly realize God's best for me? Can I identify with "exceedingly" and "abundantly" yet? I believe God is opening up our eyes daily to what He considers to be His best. We truly need to allow Him to show us His way before we make our minds up on any major decision. We should go to Him in prayer before we propose or before we say yes. Is he or she the best for us? We should seek the Lord before we go into any business covenant with anyone. Is this person the best? Are they on the up and up? Remember, God knows the heart of man (1 Sam. 16:7). We need to go into prayer before we buy that house, that car. Plain and simply said, we need to seek after God's best in everything. Everything!

God wants us to elevate in our expectations in Him. Raise the stakes. Realize your value has gone up. Once you give your life to Christ and every day from that point on, you are sacrificing your life and giving it all up for the Lord. Brother, sister, your stock has gone up! Please don't get me wrong; by no means am I suggesting with an arrogance that you are better than anybody else. No way!

God just wants some folks out there to believe for better, to see themselves worthy, to believe what God says about them. God says we are His treasure. He says we are ambassadors, and He said we are joint heirs to His kingdom (Rom. 8:17). *Believe that!* Selah and shalom.

Now unto him that is able to do exceeding abundantly above all that we ask or think, according to the power that worketh in us
—Ephesians 3:20

—Day 83—

Prayer Is the Foundation for Building

If you have been ordained by God to be a bricklayer and a kingdom builder, you are going to have to understand the power of prayer.

The first and foremost step in this process is understanding that you cannot do anything without Him. God is our source for everything. We need to seek His face daily. God wants us to establish a relationship with Him through our prayer and fellowship with Him. We have to understand that He answers prayer, and we must go before His throne and seek Him for instructions. God is faithful. He will not leave us empty handed. He will provide all that we need. His Word says if we "seek...first the kingdom of God, and his righteousness...all these things shall be added unto" us (Matt. 6:33). God knows all, and He knows the order of His plans. We have to line up with His perfect will. Everything works together for His purposes (Rom. 8:28). We have to go to Him to understand the instruction for His purpose.

No matter what you may be going through, no matter if it is good or bad, God has a way of escape for you (1 Cor. 10:13). Through your prayer He can give you joy, strength, peace, comfort, and so much more. No matter if you are shut in or you feel shut out, God can draw you into Him as you release all your understanding to Him. Allow Him today to transform your mind. Turn to Him today in prayer and fellowship, and see the work of the Lord at hand. I promise you He will not disappoint.

This is your time, right now, to increase. Increase your prayer life, and watch God increase you. Prayer is powerful in many ways. Through your prayer you can plead a case before the Lord, or you can just honor Him. God is more than able to train you and elevate you into warfare. There is much power in prayer. He can show you things in visions you would never think you would see. He will make His abundance available for you when you turn to the Lord in prayer.

Follow the example of Jesus. He prayed to His Father. In the Book of John chapter 17 He prayed for the disciples, He prayed for us, and He prayed for Himself. Take a look at the Book of Mark chapter 14:32–41. When He was in Gethsemane, Christ prayed for help from the Father to make it through to the end of His task. He prayed for God's will, not His will be done. This is how powerful prayer is. If it was good enough for the Son of God, then we should follow the King's example, and it should be good enough for us. He will do a mighty work on your behalf if you just believe in the power of prayer.

But seek ye first the kingdom of God, and his righteousness; and all these things shall be added unto you.
—Matthew 6:33

Day 84

Your Prayers Are Being Answered

God is the Father who answers prayers. He said in His Word that whatever you ask for in the name of Jesus He will do (John 14:13). We have to know when He says our "labor is not in vain" that He means just that (1 Cor. 15:58, NKJV). If we are diligently seeking the face of our Lord and Savior we can be assured our Father is moving on our behalf. The only way we can be sure of this is if we are seeking Him daily.

We have to make sure we have laid down our motives and lined them up with His will for our lives. Seek His desires and pray accordingly to what His plans are for you. Stand on His Word, and just like He says, He will come through. He wants you to know He is in control and He has the final say, whatever it is you are waiting for Him to do, whatever it is you want to see Him do. If it is a family member getting saved or a marriage being healed or you want a closer relationship with Him, He will answer your prayers.

Jesus told the disciples some deliverances take "prayer and fasting" (Mark 9:29). Don't get discouraged in the wait. Waiting brings forth perseverance. Waiting makes you strong. Waiting develops character. Waiting builds your relationship with the Lord. Listen, waiting can provide more for you than you think, and as you are waiting He is moving on your behalf. He is answering your prayer. He may not come when you want Him to or the way you want Him to come, but He is always, always, right on time. When He answers our prayers it is always "exceedingly" and "abundantly above all... we" could ever "ask or think" (Eph. 3:20). He never sleeps nor slumbers (Ps. 121:4).

Believe the report of the Lord when He says He cares for you. He is your Provider and your Deliverer. Pray that His ears are attentive to your prayer, and believe that He is listening. You must believe! Believe in His love for you, and because He loves you He is listening and answering your prayer. The key word here is *pray*. Remember, if you don't say anything, how can He hear your request? People may say, "Well, He knows everything." Yes, but He said in His Word that we "have not, because... [we] ask not" (James 4:2). We must ask, believe, and receive.

Asking is a humbling action. He wants us to come to Him like a child. He wants to be our active Father. Your natural father may have had some shortcomings, but God wants you to know He is the Father of all fathers and that you can come to Him with anything. Humility with God is a key factor in building a relationship with Him.

God is saying to you, "Knock, and I will answer" (Matt. 7:7, author's paraphrase). He wants you to come. All through the Bible He is giving you instructions and tools for you to use. He is giving you the requirements. All He wants you to do is seek Him, trust Him, and believe He is who He says He is. Then when He answers He is expecting you to do your part, and that is to be obedient. Knock at His door. He is waiting on you so He can answer your prayer.

And whatsoever ye shall ask in my name, that will I do, that the Father may be glorified in the Son..
—John 14:13

~Day 85~

Unity: Can We Come Together?

Some believe we should leave matters alone concerning the political arena, while others believe the church is not involved enough. We are the church. We should be involved in whatever is going on in our government. We have to understand who we are. We are God's government (Isa. 9:6). We represent Him and His kingdom. If we don't represent Him, who will? We have to understand we are the light and the beacons of the earth (Matt. 5:13–16).

We have to take a stand together. We must learn to put our differences aside and stand together in one accord. Can we agree? If we believe the Word of God, we agree. We cannot allow our own opinions and feelings to dictate the move of the people of God. We have to humble ourselves under His leading and allow Him to guide us, just like the Israelites—together. We must be determined not to continue in the mistakes they made. We know what became of them; everyone didn't make it into the Promised Land (Josh. 5:4–8). We have to make our minds up to put our differences aside for the common cause, and that is to see justice done on Earth. We have to see everything work in the favor of the kingdom of God.

He has called us ambassadors (2 Cor. 5:20). We are to live on "earth, as it is in heaven" (Matt. 6:10). We are to be His end-time warriors. We are His battle-ax, and we can win if we can come together. Let us be determined today to raise up Jesus and put all of our personal differences aside. Race, color, gender, and denominational differences have no place in unity. Jesus' blood is red, and He died for us all. Let us walk in boldness for righteousness and in unity. We can walk for Him in spirit and in truth.

For unto us a child is born, unto us a son is given: and the government shall be upon his shoulder: and his name shall be called Wonderful, Counsellor, The mighty God, The everlasting Father, The Prince of Peace.
—Isaiah 9:6

Day 86

Taking the Hooks of the Enemy Off Our Children

In this day and time it would be total denial for a parent not to recognize the pulling and tugging going on with our children. I would say a parent would have to be totally blind not to see the seduction of the enemy enticing our children. If you want to hear the truth, here you go: we as parents have a responsibility to raise our children. Yes, I said it. We have a responsibility to raise our children in the admonition of the Lord, no matter what they say or what the world says (Eph. 6:4). We are in the world, and not of the world (John 15:19).

I am no stranger to what is out there. I know firsthand the pressure of wanting to be accepted and wanting to please. It caused me to make a whole lot of bad decisions. Get my book *Born into Sin, Transformed into Destiny.* But in this day and age you can see clearly that things have increased as the years have gone by. My mom would say we were worse off than in her time, and I am now saying at my age that I cannot even imagine the pressure young people are under today.

Our kids are facing all kinds of temptation to have sex. Sex is everywhere you turn—on TV, on the radio, on the Internet, YouTube, Snapchat, Twitter, and sexting (sexual texting). It is everywhere. Even doing drugs has become some kind of glamorized recreation. When I was coming up, to be a crackhead was a thing of shame. What has this all come to? False religion, which tells them they can control their destiny by their thoughts. New Age witchcraft, Baphomet, and the Illuminati are just a few ideologies that have their hooks in our children.

It is time-out for playing around with the devil. We know God is in control of *everything* (1 Chron. 29:11). We as parents and the church must keep it real and keep it updated. We don't have time for playacting and/or sweeping anything under the rug. I want to see our children free, along with many others.

What is our strategy? We must study to show ourselves "approved" (2 Tim. 2:15). We must look, watch, and pay attention to what is going on and what is being said. We have to realize we are raising up a Joshua generation, and the enemy is just as determined to take our children out now as he was in killing off the young boys when he was looking for Jesus (Matt. 2). He is looking for Jesus now in us. This is his job, and no matter how much we pray, fast, and shout we are going to have to take this giant down for the count. See your children's destiny as young soldiers for God and recognize we have to be strong until they are able to fight for themselves (Josh. 1:10–18). During this time we have to train them. This is no time for you to keep your deliverance and your transformation a secret. You must walk transparent in the thing that God is doing in your life so they can understand it is a process, an everyday proposition and not a microwave solution. This is a time for the real generals to stand up and fight. We can do all things through Christ, who strengthens us (Phil. 4:13).

Don't be afraid of your children or the enemy of their souls. Stand up in the face of the enemy and tell him, "No, you cannot and will not torment my child any longer. You will not lie to them or persuade them any longer." Plead the blood of Jesus and fight the good fight of faith, all in Jesus' name.

And, ye fathers, provoke not your children to wrath: but bring them up in the nurture and admonition of the Lord.
—Ephesians 6:4

Day 81

Burn, Baby Burn

This is an awesome time of seeing firsthand the work of God in us. We have come to a place of *fire!* God is purging, pruning, and burning away everything that had a plan to hinder or delay the plans He has for us. His Word will "not return . . . void," and it will "accomplish what" it has set out to do (Isa. 55:11). This is not a time for resistance. We need to go all the way, take it on home, and finish the race.

God is only completing the work that He has started in you (Phil. 1:6). We are a work in progress. Every artist has an eye for the imperfections that no one else sees. It is up to the artist to complete the work to perfection, that it may be displayed to their standards for the world to view. It is viewing time. God is preparing His people for the open view. Some of you are being catapulted in arenas that nobody but God put you in. It is time for open viewing. God has raised "a standard" for us in the face of our enemy (Isa. 59:19). This is the time for the work that is needed for the elevation. We had to go through some things to get where we are going. So I say burn, baby, burn; burn away all that flesh. I will see You at the next level.

Purge me, Lord, in the name of Jesus. Take us higher in You, Lord, in Jesus' name.

God is purging, pruning, and burning away everything that had a plan to hinder or delay the plans He has for us.

Day 88

What Time Is It?

Do you know what time it is? God is lining us up with His time. We must understand what season we are in to receive the blessings of the Lord. He desires for us to receive the abundance that He has for us in the seasons of outpour. This is the time to ask God, What season are we in, Lord? We must surrender our understanding to His. We must line up with His timespan. We must pray for wisdom and the Issachar anointing (1 Chron. 12:32). Are we in a season of power? A season of wealth? We need to know what season He is leading us into so that we can receive the best of the Lord. Receive your blessing today, and be blessed in the timing of God.

And of the children of Issachar, which were men that had understanding of the times, to know what Israel ought to do.
—1 Chronicles 12:32a

Day 89

One Day at a Time

T*rusting is challenging for most*, but God wants us to trust Him with everything. When we trust Him God truly shows Himself mighty. He "is able to do exceedingly abundantly above all that we ask or think" (Eph. 3:20). He provides just what we need, when we need it. He gives us a daily portion. So why worry? Don't you know worrying adds nothing to your life (Luke 12:25, NKJV)? It only steals your time and your peace.

No matter what you're facing today, choose to trust God. He is your Father, and He cares about everything concerning you. Remain in the now! It is your "*now* faith" that moves mountains.

> Now faith is the substance of things hoped for, the evidence of things not seen.
>
> —Hebrews 11:1

Be encouraged, and believe God today. He will provide! It is a promise from Him, a promise that will not return to Him void (Isa. 55:11).

We are on a one-day-at-a-time journey. Pray for God to give you peace and the strength only He can give you. Once you get it, fight with everything inside you to remain. Trust God no matter what. He will take care of it all for you. Just trust Him.

Trust God no matter what. He will take care of it all for you.

⊸Day 90⊸

You Are a True Warrior

There is nothing you can't do in the will of God. You "can do all things through Christ," who strengthens you (Phil. 4:13). It is your time!

You have made it through this spiritual boot camp successfully! In the last ninety days you have overcome some major difficulties with great victory. You are a winner! The enemy is defeated! The tools you have learned from this devotional have changed your perception. You have grown and now see things differently. You have the strength to move forward with truth and great expectation in God, so move forward. Take your next steps in faith and conviction. This devotional shouldn't be the end of your time of growth with the Lord. Make it the beginning of a new season of transformation!

I pray for God's protection over your life and everything that concerns you. I am believing Father for more spiritual growth and elevation in your life, that He will direct you and keep you. I pray God will increase your prayer life and for Him to give you revelation by revealing more of Himself to you. May He continue to transform your mind, and may you become more like Him. Have your way, heavenly Father, in Jesus' name, Amen.

Be blessed and go forth knowing you are a warrior!

Be blessed and go forth knowing you are a warrior!

About the Author

Dr. Gina R. Prince is a chosen and yielded vessel of God who is totally committed to spreading a life-changing message of hope to all she encounters. She is a noted pastor, health and fitness expert, radio personality, and author based in the Washington, D.C., area.

Dr. Gina, as she is affectionately and widely known, operates in the office of apostle. She was the former overseer of Gospel Truth Ministries International–East Gate Church in Washington, DC. By the direction of the Holy Spirit she was ordained July 7, 2004. Since that time Apostle Prince has united with other leaders locally and abroad through prayer and intercession to tear down the kingdom of darkness.

As a defender of the gospel, Dr. Gina's ministry is one of deliverance, intimacy with God, and learning the truth of God's Word. Apostle Prince is a graduate of Word Bible College/MNC, where she obtained a bachelor's degree in intercession and a master's in Christian counseling. Apostle Prince also obtained her doctorate degree in theology from Spoken Word College in 2013. She appeared on the cable show *Celebrate* with Bishop Gary Davis on Total Christian Television, where Gospel Truth Ministries was nationally introduced. Also, the ministry was locally introduced and she was interviewed by Esau Davis (better known as C.O.) on 96.1 FM *The Beat* radio station in Charlotte, North Carolina. Dr. Gina labors in faith regularly with ministries from Michigan to Florida.

A native of Detroit, Michigan, Dr. Gina achieved a measure of athleticism in high school, which subsequently laid the foundation for the destiny God had already ordained. Today she is a certified Tae Bo instructor, personal trainer, and health and fitness expert. She stands strong in her conviction that our mind, body, and soul equate to wholeness in the sight of God. Apostle

Prince is the author of *Born Into Sin, Transformed Into Destiny,* her testimony of how God transformed her life. She is also the host of *Dr. Gina's Radio Chat,* which airs on BBS Radio, Station #1, on Wednesday at 11:00 am EST. Dr. Gina is currently a guest columnist for streamingfaith.com.

Contact the Author

Email: drginarprince@gmail.com

Facebook: DrGina R. Prince

Twitter and Instagram: @GinaRPrince

Tumblr: DRGinaRPrince

Websites: drginaprince.com, myhealthnsoul.com, and TheKeysAgainsttheEnemy.com

Podcasts: For more devotionals, listen to Dr. Gina Prince's podcast, *The Keys Against the Enemy*, on the Charisma Podcast Network. Download on CharismaPodcastNetwork.com, iTunes, or Google Play Music.